WELL BUI

MYCENAE

The Helleno-British Excavations
Within the Citadel at Mycenae, 1959–1969

W. D. Taylour, E. B. French, K. A. Wardle

FASCICULE 7

The Prehistoric Cemetery:
Pre-Mycenaean and Early Mycenaean Graves

M. Alden

Published and distributed by
Oxbow Books, Park End Place, Oxford OX1 1HN
Phone: (+44) 01865-241249, Fax: (+44) 01865-794449
Email: oxbow@oxbowbooks.com

Distributed in North America by
The David Brown Book Company
PO Box 511, Oakville, CT 06779
Phone: (860) 945-9329, Fax: (860) 945-9468
Email: david.brown.bk.co@snet.net

Website address
www.oxbowbooks.com

ISBN 1 84217 018 X

Printed in Great Britain at
The Short Run Press, Exeter

CONTENTS

TEXT

TEXT ILLUSTRATIONS

Figures

Plates

(*b*) **PC'39 Grave III**, LH I pottery: 39-239 goblet with one high-swung handle (*left*); 39-238 askos with loop handle (*centre*); 39-242 small jug with cutaway neck and loop handle (*right*). 39A44.

FICHE

The individual graves and their contents:

FICHE ILLUSTRATIONS

Plans

FOREWORD

The burials which have been found on and around the citadel at Mycenae reflect almost every phase of the site's history from Early Helladic to Hellenistic. Some of the earliest of these graves, which date to the Middle Helladic and early Mycenaean periods, cluster on the lower western and northwestern slopes of the acropolis hill, within and without the later fortification wall. The graves in Grave Circle A, excavated by Schliemann in 1876, were the first and remain the richest group of graves to be discovered, but it was Chr. Tsountas who realised from the presence of simpler graves in the area that the Circle belonged to an extensive early cemetery — the Prehistoric Cemetery. Following this lead A. J. B. Wace was encouraged to carry out tests in the 1920's followed by the systematic investigations which took place between 1939 and 1953. During this later period the second rich group of graves, Grave Circle B, was found and excavated by I. Papademetriou and his colleagues, towards the western end of the area. Exploration of the levels below parts of the Citadel House Area and to the south of Tsountas House (W. D. Taylour in 1968, 1969 and G. E. Mylonas in 1973) revealed more graves to add to the total of well over 100 already known from the area as a whole.

In 1978 Lord William Taylour entrusted the study of the new burials to Maureen Alden, who had recently completed a PhD dissertation entitled *Bronze Age Population Fluctuations in the Argolid from the Evidence of Mycenaean Tombs* (see Alden 1981). This study has been enlarged to form the basis of the present fascicule, including full details of the burial practices and finds from as many of the burials as possible, but especially those from Wace's excavations from 1939 to 1953, and Taylour's in 1968 and 1969. As full an account as possible of the cemetery has been brought together in this fascicule, using all available site notebooks and archival material as well as the full publication of the 1939 excavations and the preliminary reports of differing detail on the seasons from 1950–53. Thus it is possible for the first time to gain a clear picture of this early cemetery and of the finds made in both richer and poorer graves — a picture which for the moment is almost the only one we have of the community which occupied the citadel of Mycenae before and at the beginning of the Mycenaean period. Though Middle Helladic pottery is copious throughout the site, remains of early structures on the citadel which date to this period are so scanty that they give little idea of the size of this community, its wealth and prosperity or its external connections. Although none of the finds in the graves outside the Grave Circles can match those of the Royal burials in them, their number confirms the presence of a substantial community and the finds suggest a general level of prosperity. With a wider perspective Maureen Alden has been able to expand our knowledge of the grave types and burial customs, of the range of grave offerings and markers and of the extent of re-use in the early Mycenaean cemeteries of the Argolid, as well as at Mycenae itself.

Maureen Alden has also reviewed the available evidence of physical anthropology gathered by Lawrence Angel and others — our only direct evidence of the character of the inhabitants of Mycenae.

The pottery catalogue on fiche and CD has been compiled from the original registration cards, therefore descriptions given are those as identified at the time of excavation, and have not been corrected. Where allocated, new Mycenae Museum (MM) numbers have been entered in the catalogue. Objects that have not yet received a Mycenae Museum number retain their old Nauplia Museum numbers in brackets.

We are grateful to the Trustees of the Mediterranean Archaeological Trust for their support of the work necessary to prepare this fascicule for publication and to Linda Witherill for a grant to support work relating specifically to the analysis and full publication of graves discovered by A. J. B. Wace. We are indebted to Graham Norrie for preparing all the photographic and digital prints needed for the text and supporting data and especially for his ingenious montage (Plate 1) of panoramic photographs of the Citadel taken specifically by EBF at different times of day to show the extent and features of the cemetery. Diana Wardle, who has prepared the cover design, and Rayna Andrew, who has once more undertaken the preparation of camera-ready copy, also richly deserve our special thanks. With the publication of the previous Fascicule (10: *The Temple Complex*) we undertook, with the assistance of Trevor King and other staff at Bell and Howell, the preparation of the supporting data in CD-ROM format in addition to the microfiche, in order to make this information as readily available as possible. We have done the same for this Fascicule but, *in addition*, we have included the data provided on fiche for Fascicules already published (1: *The Excavations*; 21: *Mycenaean Pictorial Pottery*; 27: *Ground Stone*; 36: *The Hellenistic Dye-works*). It is our intention to continue this practice, consolidating the dataset on CD-ROM with each fascicule published, so that eventually 2 or 3 CDs will contain all the supporting data in logical groups, to provide a powerful, and so far unique research tool for Mycenaean archaeology.

KAW/EBF Sept. 2000

INTRODUCTION

The text section of this account of the Prehistoric Cemetery gives a brief narrative of the excavation of the cemetery together with a summary of the excavated areas. Inside the fortification walls the areas excavated are designated by the letters originally allocated to them by Professor Wace in *BSA* 45, 206–7. Outside the fortification walls the areas of the Prehistoric Cemetery correspond to the areas excavated in 1939, 1950, 1952, and 1953, and to more recent excavations by the Archaeological Society of Athens. An account of the MH settlement at Mycenae and of the Prehistoric Cemetery in the context of other cemeteries of similar date is followed by a summary of the graves excavated in Γ, the Citadel House Area, the main concern of this series. Finally there is a brief discussion of the skeletal evidence as reported by J. Lawrence Angel. Those who require fuller information should consult the fiche catalogue for details of each area of the excavation. The catalogue uses the same letters and other designations as the text section for the areas of the cemetery, and provides a full account of each grave and its contents, together with details of deposits thought to be from disturbed graves.

ACKNOWLEDGEMENTS

My thanks are due to The Queen's University of Belfast for leave in the autumn of 1999 and for a grant to cover the cost of making the drawings from notebooks. I am grateful to the British Academy for funding a research visit to London and to an editorial conference in Birmingham.
Lord William Taylour supplied me with a great deal of information which forms the basis of this publication. It would never have appeared without the excavators, Maureen Barry, Angela Care Evans, Joost Crouwel, Lisa French, Dorothea Gray, Vronwy Hankey, Sinclair Hood, Alan Hunter, George Huxley, Marigold Pakenham-Walsh, Nicholas Postgate, Ingrid Strøm, John Watson, and Professors Tsountas, Wace, Papademetriou, Mylonas and Iakovides. Lisa French corresponded with me on points of detail for many years, and provided supportive advice and encouragement. Without her this publication would never have seen the light of day. Diana Wardle advised me on the detail of drawings and plans, and I am deeply grateful both to her and to Ken Wardle for editorial guidance and support. With unfailing efficiency Rayna Andrew produced photographs and other material from the archives: she is also responsible for the final layout of the fiche pages and adjustments to the text. David Heylings of the Anatomy Department at Queen's was kind enough to advise me on the interpretation of Angel's reports on skeletal material. Olga Krzyszkowska and Helen Brock provided much helpful guidance and advice, and Sue Willetts and other library staff at the Joint Library of the Hellenic and Roman Societies provided assistance that went way beyond the call of duty. Maura Pringle, Senior Cartographer at Queen's, produced the beautiful fold-out plan and the small area plans: no words can express my gratitude for her skill and great forbearance in the face of myriad alterations and corrections. James Davis, Graphic Designer in the Audio-Visual unit at Queen's is responsible for the drawings of graves taken from excavation notebooks: I am immensely grateful to him for his skill and patience in completing this exacting task. I shall never be able to convey my thanks to my husband, Michael Allen, for his tolerance and unswerving loyalty as this work was brought slowly to fruition.

PLATE 1

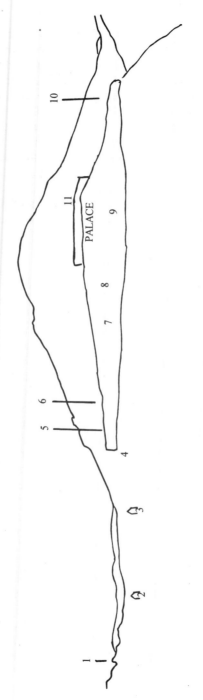

Panoramic montage of the Citadel with accompanying diagram indicating specific features of the Prehistoric Cemetery.

1	Grave Circle B	5	Lion Gate	9	Hellenistic Tower
2	Tomb of Clytemnestra	6	Grave Circle A	10	House Zeta
3	Tomb of Atreus	7	Ramp House/House of the Warrior Vase	11	Palace
4	PCE	8	South House Annex		

THE PREHISTORIC CEMETERY

The Prehistoric Cemetery at Mycenae provides our most coherent glimpse of the Middle Helladic period at Mycenae. It comprises not only the prestigious burials with dazzling displays of grave objects found in the wealthiest graves of Grave Circles A and B, but also a whole host of lesser graves spanning the period from MH to LH II. Many of these burials have been disturbed, either by the Bronze Age practice of re-using graves or in later building operations, but others have been found intact. The cemetery has been the object of investigation and study for more than a hundred years, and many publications on its graves have already appeared, especially on the wealthy burials of the two Grave Circles. However, this is the first attempt to draw together all the available information about the cemetery, published and unpublished, and to synthesize the evidence it provides for burial practices at Mycenae in the period MH–LH II. The excavations of Schliemann in 1876 uncovered not only five of the Shaft Graves in Grave Circle A, but also a number of smaller graves on the eastern side of the circle. These smaller graves, which were never satisfactorily recorded at the time of excavation, appear to have been characteristic of many of the graves of the Prehistoric Cemetery; they dated to MH and contained little apart from the burial. The smaller graves were already in existence at the time of the construction of Grave Circle A, but were unknown to, or ignored by, the founders of the shaft graves. Grave Circle B also contained early graves disregarded by the founders of the circle (Dickinson 1977, 40, 46). Until the establishment of the Grave Circles in the later stages of the Middle Helladic period, the Prehistoric Cemetery at Mycenae was very similar to other cemeteries of similar date in the region: it may be compared with MH– LH II cemeteries at Lerna, Prosymna, Argos, Corinth, and Asine.

The Prehistoric Cemetery is situated on the lower slopes of the acropolis at Mycenae on its western side: on the north it probably extends as far as the Postern Gate and at the south graves belonging to the cemetery have been found in the area of the West and East Houses beside the ancient road to the Citadel (Pls. 1–2). The cemetery extends both outside and inside the fortification walls, over a large area of soft rock which appears immediately to the west of the Ramp leading from the Lion Gate to the palace. This soft rock is easily cut for graves. Some graves from the Prehistoric Cemetery must have been visible in the second century AD, because Pausanias alludes to the local stories about them in his account of Mycenae:

Μυκηνῶν δὲ ἐν τοῖς ἐρειπίοις κρήνη τέ ἐστι καλουμένη Περσεία, καὶ Ἀτρέως καὶ τῶν παίδων ὑπόγαια οἰκοδομήματα, ἔνθα οἱ θησαυροί σφισι τῶν χρημάτων ἦσαν. τάφος δὲ ἐστι μὲν Ἀτρέως, εἰσὶ δὲ καὶ ὅσους σὺν Ἀγαμέμνονι ἐπανήκοντας ἐξ Ἰλίου δειπνίσας κατεφόνευσεν Αἴγισθος. τοῦ μὲν δὴ Κασσάνδρας μνήματος ἀμφισβητοῦσι Λακεδαιμονίων οἱ περὶ Ἀμύκλας οἰκοῦντες· ἕτερον δὲ ἐστιν Ἀγαμέμνονος, τὸ δὲ Εὐρυμέδοντος τοῦ ἡνιόχου, καὶ Τελεδάμου τὸ αὐτὸ καὶ Πέλοπος, τούτους γὰρ τεκεῖν διδύμους Κασσάνδραν φασί, νηπίους δὲ ἔτι ὄντας ἐπικατέσφαξε τοῖς γονεῦσιν Αἴγισθος,... Κλυταιμνήστρα δὲ ἐτάφη καὶ Αἴγισθος ὀλίγον ἀπωτέρω τοῦ τείχους, ἐντὸς δὲ ἀπηξιώθησαν, ἔνθα Ἀγαμέμνων τε αὐτὸς ἔκειτο καὶ οἱ σὺν ἐκείνῳ φονευθέντες.

In the ruins of Mycenae is a spring called Perseia, and the underground dwellings of Atreus and his sons, where the treasuries of their goods were. There is the grave of Atreus and those whom Aegisthus feasted and murdered on their return from Troy with Agamemnon. The Spartans who dwell round Amyclae dispute the grave of Cassandra, but another tomb is Agamemnon's, another that of Eurymedon, his charioteer, and a single grave holds Teledamos and Pelops, for they say that Cassandra bore them as twins, and while they were still infants Aegisthus slaughtered them with their parents… Clytemnestra and Aegisthus were buried a little further from the wall. They were not thought worthy to lie inside, where lay Agamemnon himself and those murdered with him.

Pausanias 2. 16. 5
(translation by M. Alden)

The tradition known to Pausanias appears to be based on a passage in the *Odyssey* where the ghost of Agamemnon describes his fate:

ἀλλά μοι Αἴγισθος τεύξας θάνατόν τε μόρον τε
ἔκτα σὺν οὐλομένῃ ἀλόχῳ, οἶκόνδε καλέσσας
δειπνίσσας, ὥς τίς τε κατέκτανε βοῦν ἐπὶ φάτνῃ.
ὣς θάνον οἰκτίστῳ θανάτῳ· περὶ δ' ἄλλοι ἑταῖροι
νωλεμέως κτείνοντο, σύες ὣς ἀργιόδοντες
οἵ ῥά τ' ἐν ἀφνειοῦ ἀνδρὸς μέγα δυναμένοιο
ἢ γάμῳ ἢ ἐράνῳ ἢ εἰλαπίνῃ τεθαλυίῃ.
ἤδη μὲν πολέων φόνῳ ἀνδρῶν αντεβόλησας,
μουνὰξ κτεινομένων καὶ ἐνὶ κρατερῇ ὑσμίνῃ·
ἀλλά κε κεῖνα μάλιστα ἰδὼν ὀλοφύραο θυμῷ,
ὡς ἀμφὶ κρητῆρα τραπέζας τε πληθούσας
κείμεθ' ἐνὶ μεγάρῳ, δάπεδον δ' ἅπαν αἵματι θῦεν.
οἰκτροτάτην δ' ἤκουσα ὄπα Πριάμοιο θυγατρός,
Κασσάνδρης, τὴν κτεῖνε Κλυταιμνήστρη δολόμητις
ἀμφ' ἐμοί· αὐτὰρ ἐγὼ ποτὶ γαίῃ χεῖρας ἀείρων
βάλλον ἀποθνήσκων περὶ φασγάνῳ· ἡ δὲ κυνῶπις
νοσφίσατ' οὐδέ μοι ἔτλη ἰόντι περ εἰς Ἀΐδαο
χερσὶ κατ' ὀφθαλμοὺς ἑλέειν σύν τε στόμ' ἐρεῖσαι.

But Aegisthus, fashioning death and doom for me
killed me in league with my accursed wife, when he had invited me home
and feasted me, as one kills an ox at the manger.
So I died a most pitiable death. And without pause,
they killed my other companions around me as savage-tusked pigs
are slaughtered in the house of a rich man with great power
either for a wedding, or a feast, or a lavish banquet.
In your time you have met with the murder, singly, of many men
killed in the strong din of battle,
but you would have pitied these things most in your heart,

seeing how we lay in the hall around the wine bowl and the groaning tables,
and all the floor ran with blood.
And I heard the most pitiful voice of the daughter of Priam,
Cassandra, whom guileful Clytemnestra killed
with me. But I lifted up my hands and beat upon the ground
as I died on the sword. But the bitch
departed, nor, although I was going to the house of Hades,
did she deign to close my eyes or close my mouth.

Odyssey 11. 409–26 (see also *Odyssey* 24. 95–7).

(translation by M. Alden)

Pausanias' account retains the sequence of events found in this passage from the *Odyssey*: in both accounts Aegisthus kills Agamemnon when he has feasted him. Pausanias' account of the local tradition about the graves led Schliemann to identify the five Shaft Graves he excavated in 1876 in Grave Circle A inside the fortification walls as the graves of Agamemnon and his followers, murdered by Clytemnestra and Aegisthus. It soon became clear that the five Shaft Graves had nothing to do with Agamemnon and his returning army, but Schliemann's excavations paved the way for a succession of later excavations which have revealed an extensive cemetery of which Grave Circle A and Grave Circle B are only a part.

Professor Tsountas believed that a number of smaller graves would eventually be found outside Grave Circle A, making up an entire cemetery together with the graves contained inside the Grave Circle. He drew attention to the graves beneath the houses to the south of Grave Circle A, describing them as 'oblong pits hollowed in the soft rock, but of little depth, doubtless because the rock here lay below the surface' (Tsountas and Manatt 1897, 114). Some of these pits lay beneath the House of the Warrior Vase: they are treated in this publication as section H. The Golden Treasure came from just south of Grave Circle A.

In conversation with Professor Wace, Tsountas often expressed his conviction that the Prehistoric Cemetery would be found to have extended outside the Lion Gate and the fortification walls, that is to say to the north and west of Grave Circle A (*BSA* 45, 207). In notes dating to 1955 Wace records a ruined grave found by the Anastelosis Department in 1954 close to the north-west corner of the tower or bastion which guards the approach to the Lion Gate (*BSA* 50, 190). In 1955 Dr. Papademetriou found two graves about eight metres west of the corner of the bastion, close to the fortification wall. In the same year he also found two other graves west of the tile pavement lying outside the fortification wall at the point where inside the fortification wall lay Grave Circle A. All these graves demonstrate the continuity of the two parts of the Prehistoric Cemetery, that within the fortification wall, of which Grave Circle A is, so to speak, the kernel, and the part outside the fortifications to the north-west. This all helps to show that Tsountas was right in his belief that the Prehistoric Cemetery, of which Grave Circle A was the most prestigious part, covered a large area both inside and outside the fortification walls. The graves found in 1954 and 1955 prove that the fortification wall was built through the middle of the Prehistoric Cemetery when it was disused.

The exploration around Grave Circle A within the fortification walls near the Lion Gate begun in 1920 resulted in the discovery of several further groups of graves, leading to the conclusion that a Prehistoric cemetery, in use from Middle Helladic until LH II had lain on the hillside in this area before the fortifications were constructed. In time, the Shaft Graves of Grave Circles

A and B were constructed to contain the burials of particular groups, although the oldest burials discovered in the area of each Grave Circle were probably already in existence when the enclosures were built. The whole space occupied by the fortifications, the Granary, Grave Circle A, and the houses immediately to the south of the latter is marked by the presence of soft rock in which the Shaft Graves were dug. On the east this area is bounded by a line drawn from the east side of the Lion Gate and under the Ramp to the east side of the Ramp House. Eastwards of this line rises the slope of hard limestone of which most of the citadel is composed (*BSA* 25, pl. 1). Westwards the hill slopes downwards, and wherever the rock has been exposed, either within or without the fortification walls, it is the same soft rock as that of the Shaft Graves. The dividing line between the soft rock and the hard limestone can be seen outside the Lion Gate at the foot of that sector of the Citadel wall which runs from the east side of the Lion Gate northwards to the north-west angle of the enceinte and is constructed in ashlar work in conglomerate. This is the nearest area to the summit of the Citadel where it was possible to dig out graves in the rock.

PLATE 2

Aerial view of the western slope of the acropolis showing the extent of the Prehistoric Cemetery.
Photograph by J. Wilson Myers and Eleanor E. Myers.

PLATE 3

Citadel House Area, Γ21/22 under excavation, 1966.

SUMMARY OF THE EXCAVATED AREAS

WITHIN THE FORTIFICATION WALLS

On the west side of the Citadel we have the following groups (*BSA* 45, 206; Wace 1949, 61):

A (Fig. 1; fiche 104–10)
The Six Shaft Graves, five of which were found by Schliemann and the sixth by Stamatakes. (The numbering of these graves established by Stamatakes is observed by the National Museum at Athens and all publications subsequent to those of Schliemann, who had used a different system of numbering.)

B (Fig. 1; fiche 111–13)
The skeletons found by Schliemann on the slope of the rock east of Shaft Grave III. With these he says he found four Middle Helladic vases.[1] It is sometimes thought that these skeletons and vases come from MH graves which were destroyed when the Third Shaft Grave was dug (Karo 1930–33, 16). It seems more likely, however, that these burials were intact when Schliemann found them. The vases were unbroken and Schliemann implies that the skeletons were complete, although the bones and skulls were so much perished that the skulls could not be extracted entire. Had the bones and skulls lain in disorder, so acute an observer as Schliemann would certainly have noticed the circumstance.

C (Fig. 1; fiche 114–16)
The four graves found by Stamatakes in the east part of the Grave Circle.

C* (Fig. 1; fiche 117–23)
To these graves in the area of Grave Circle A should be added one further shaft grave, here designated **C* 1955 Shaft Grave** (*PAE* 1955, 228–9 and fig. 6; 1957, 105–8 and pl. 46β), in the north-east part of the circle, near the entrance, and partially underlying the inner ring of slabs.

Also in the area of Grave Circle A were two pit graves (*PAE* 1957, 108), here designated **C* 1955 Pit Grave 1**, a small pit of irregular shape south of, and very close to **C* 1955 Shaft Grave**; and **C* 1955 Pit Grave 2**, an irregular pit at the south-east corner of Shaft Grave VI. These two pit graves were both found empty.

In the space at the foot of the supporting wall of the ring of slabs of Grave Circle A on the west there is an artificial cutting in the rock now filled with small stones as a bedding for the base of the fortification wall (*BSA* 25, 105 pl. 1, 63; *BSA* 45, 207). This cutting might conceivably be that of a grave which was discovered and destroyed when the wall was being built.

D (Fig. 1; fiche 124–37)
The plundered Shaft Grave, probably of LH II date, found underneath the floor of the east basement of the Granary in 1920 (*BSA* 25, 55ff). Since the gold discs, which probably once adorned a dress, suggest that there was a woman buried in this grave, and the pieces of boar's tusk from a helmet suggest a man, it may have been the grave of a husband and wife of a noble family.

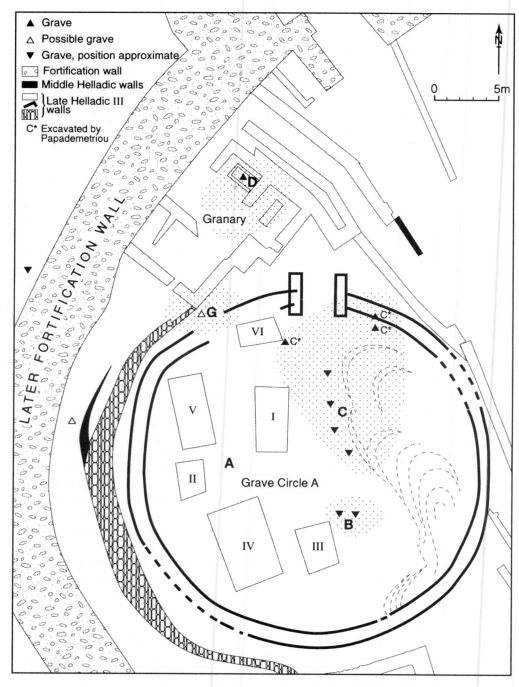

Legend:
- ▲ Grave
- △ Possible grave
- ▼ Grave, position approximate
- Fortification wall
- Middle Helladic walls
- Late Helladic III walls
- C* Excavated by Papademetriou

0 5m

LATER FORTIFICATION WALL

▲D

Granary

△G

VI

▲C*

▲C*

▲C*

V

I

C*

II

A

Grave Circle A

IV

III

B

Fig. 1.   Areas A–D and G: graves in the vicinity of Grave Circle A.

E (Fig. 2; fiche 139–53)
The three certain Middle Helladic Graves found below the Ramp House in 1920–3 (*BSA* 25, 76, 118), and the three possible graves found at the same time beneath the same house (*BSA* 25, 78). The latter are shallow rock cuttings under the north wall of the megaron of that house. They were found empty, but may well be graves which had been disturbed when the house was built. In 1960 a further grave and two cuttings which might have been graves were discovered, bringing the total number of graves under the Ramp House to four, together with five cuttings which might have been graves.

F (Fig. 3; fiche 154–61)
The Middle Helladic Grave below the South House (*BSA* 25, 94; Pl. 12*a*). Only in the East Room was a test pit sunk right down to the rock. Other graves may remain unexcavated under the South House.

G (Fig. 1; fiche 162–6)
Outside the Grave Circle between Shaft Grave VI and the West Basement of the Granary there was apparently another rock-cut grave. The rock seems to be cut vertically for a depth of about 1.25–1.40 m where there is a levelled space. There are traces of stone walling on three sides. This was first explored by Tsountas, then by Wace in 1920, and in 1948 by Papademetriou. Owing to these successive disturbances it is now difficult to be sure about the shape of this probable grave.

Golden Treasure (Fig. 2; fiche 167–76)
Another possible grave was the Golden Treasure (H. Thomas 1938–39, 65–87 and pls. 27–8) found just to the south of the Grave Circle by Schliemann's surveyor.

H (Fig. 2; 177–98, 203–213)
The sixteen graves discovered in 1950 beneath the House of the Warrior Vase.

Γ Citadel House Area (Figs. 3 and 5; fiche 214–81)
Eighteen graves were found during the Helleno-British excavations of 1966–8. They date from late MH to LH IIB. In addition, two large storage pots next to wall **pe** on the west side may perhaps have contained burials. Some of the small walls in the area were thought to enclose the cemetery area.
  Two further graves were excavated by Professor Mylonas, one under Room xxv (T7) on the south side of the Room with the Fresco (*PAE* 1973, 101), and one further south under the floor of Z3 in the buildings of the SW Quarter (*PAE* 1973, 103, 104 fig. 2, and pl. 117b). Other graves may very well remain unexcavated under the LH III structures.

M (Fold-out plan; fiche 283–7)
Two graves were found in 1963 on the north-west slope of the acropolis, between the Lion Gate and the palace: the first, the burial of a middle-aged man, is dated to the MH period, and the second burial, of a small child, is dated to Late Helladic (*PAE* 1963, 102). Two MH burials in jars were found further to the east (*PAE* 1963, 103).

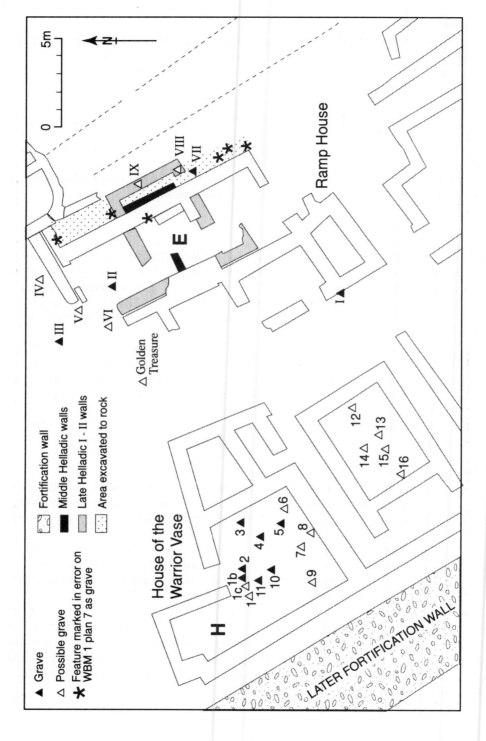

Fig. 2.   Areas E and H: graves in the vicinity of the House of the Warrior Vase and the Ramp House.

10

N (Fold-out plan; fiche 288–9)

One grave of MH date was found under House N to the left of, and above the Lion Gate (*PAE* 1984, 236 and pl. 143a).

OUTSIDE THE FORTIFICATION WALLS TO THE N AND W

A much smaller area of soft rock similar to that of the Shaft Graves, just outside the Postern Gate, was explored in 1939 (*BSA* 45, 204–6) and several rock cuttings, probably plundered graves, were found, but the pottery in them was mostly Hellenistic. Only a little Mycenaean ware (LH III) was found. However, the following areas were examined for graves belonging to the Prehistoric Cemetery (see Fig. 4).

Area 1 (Fig. 4; Pls. 4, 5*b*; fiche 304–89)

Just below the Lion Gate to the north-west Tsountas had cleared a small space round some later walls and revealed the surface of the soft rock not far below them. In 1939, following a suggestion made by Tsountas, this area to the north-west of the Lion Gate outside the walls was explored and fifteen graves found there all cut in the soft rock. These graves were numbered **I–XV** (*BSA* 45, 208 f).

Area 2

This trench, about 15.00 m long and 2.00 m wide, was dug in 1939 through the lower part, the tail, of Schliemann's dump. Below the original surface level the trench was carried down to the rock in the hope that traces of tombs might be found. The bedrock is the same soft friable rock of which the whole of this side of the citadel hill consists from the Lion Gate westwards, and it slopes generally from east to west. In view of the discovery of the prehistoric graves to the north in Area 1, it was not considered worthwhile to open out this trench or to try to trace further the walls discovered in it (*BSA* 45, 222–4).

SE Extension Area 1 (Fig. 4; fiche 403–26)

In 1950 nine more graves (**XVI–XXIV**) were found. Most had been plundered when later buildings were erected above the disused cemetery, but in one grave (**XXIII**), that of an adolescent, three characteristic Middle Helladic vases were found intact (Pl. 11). In this area was found a model of a figure-of-eight shield in ivory (*JHS* 71, 254–7).

Areas 3 and 4 (Fig. 4; Pls. 6, 7*a*; fiche 427–98, 503–98, 603–23)

Ten further graves (**XXV–XXXIV**) of MH date (Pl. 10*d*) were excavated in 1952 in the south-east extension, to the west and north-west of the area excavated in 1939.

In addition many fragments of good painted pottery were found in the area, presumably from graves of LH I or LH II date which had been plundered when the cemetery was abandoned on the building of the Lion Gate and fortification walls.

More important than all these were the remains of the contents of what must have been a rich LH II tomb with a remarkable group of ivories. The tomb might have been the pit found empty in 1939 just to the west of **Grave X** (*BSA* 45, 209 fig. 2).

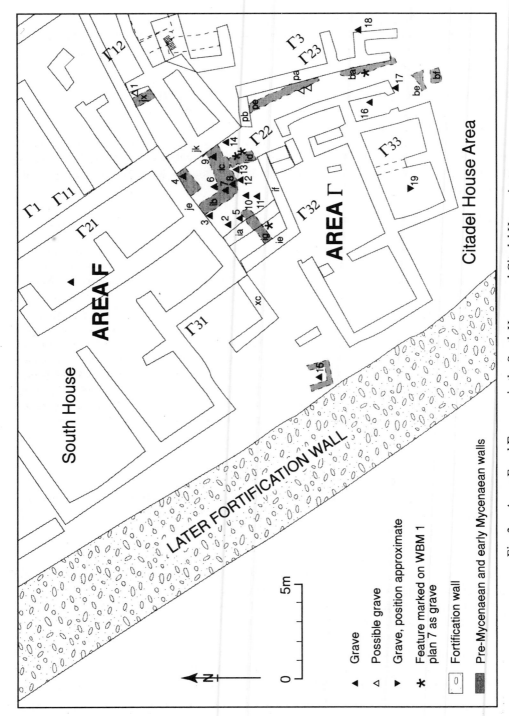

Fig. 3. Areas F and Γ: graves in the South House and Citadel House Area.

Southern Sector 1953 (Fig. 4; Pl. 8; fiche 624–47, 649)
In 1953 a section was dug to the south of the ivory deposit discovered in 1952, but the ivory deposit did not extend in this direction. Five more Middle Helladic graves were found (**XXXV–XXXVIII, XL**) (*BSA* 49, 232–3).

Northern Sector 1953 (Fig. 4; fiche 650–71)
To the north a section was excavated immediately to the north of the area dug in 1952. Only one MH grave (**XLI**) was found.

Two pits found under the Perseia Fountain House might have been plundered shaft graves of MH type (*BSA* 48, 25 and pl. 12). The first, π, is a shallow rectangular pit 1.40 m long, 0.80 m wide, and cut 0.15 m deep below the surface of the rock. The second, o, is a deeper rectangular cutting (see Fold-out plan).

Graves west of the Acropolis 1954–5 (*PAE* 1955, 223–5, and fig. 2) (Fold-out plan and Plan 16; fiche 703–13)
In 1954 the Anastelosis Department found a ruined grave (**Anastelosis Grave**), possibly of sub-Mycenaean date close to the north-west corner of the tower or bastion which guards the approach to the Lion Gate (*BSA* 50, 190 and unpublished notes by Professor Wace. See also French and Iakovides, forthcoming. This grave is not shown on the Fold-out plan). In 1955 Dr. Papademetriou found another grave (**1955 Grave 3**) about eight metres west of the corner of the bastion.[2] He also found two other graves west of a tile pavement discovered outside the fortification wall just at the place where, inside the walls, lay Grave Circle A. These two graves were both small shaft graves probably used for the burial of children. One (**PAE 1955 Grave 1**) lay about 0.70 m west of the tile pavement and about 2 m from the base of the fortification wall. The other (**PAE 1955 Grave 2**) lay somewhat further west. The two graves were of similar dimensions (0.75 m long; 0.48 m wide; 0.40 m deep). Both had been disturbed, but at the bottom of **PAE 1955 Grave 2** was a small alabastron of LH II date, decorated on the body with a beautiful ivy-leaf design (Papademetriou, unpublished handwritten notes; published information in *PAE* 1955, 223–5 and fig. 2).

1961 (Fold-out plan; fiche 714)
At the base of the west face of the fortification wall immediately to the west of the 'Granary', an MH grave was discovered cut into the rock. It had been emptied during the construction of the fortification wall (*PAE* 1961, 158–9).

Grave Circle B (Fold-out plan)
Twenty-six graves, including fourteen true shaft graves have been excavated in this Grave Circle discovered outside the fortification walls in 1951 (Mylonas 1972–3). I have used Professor Mylonas' (1972–3) full publication of this Grave Circle. There is no fiche section on Grave Circle B as I have no additional information to offer.

The Tomb of Aegisthus
There is evidence to suggest that the construction of the Tomb of Aegisthus should be dated to early LH II. The tholos is probably the latest of the first constructional group and exhibits features of the second group, such as a relieving triangle, blocked on the inside (for the constructional

13

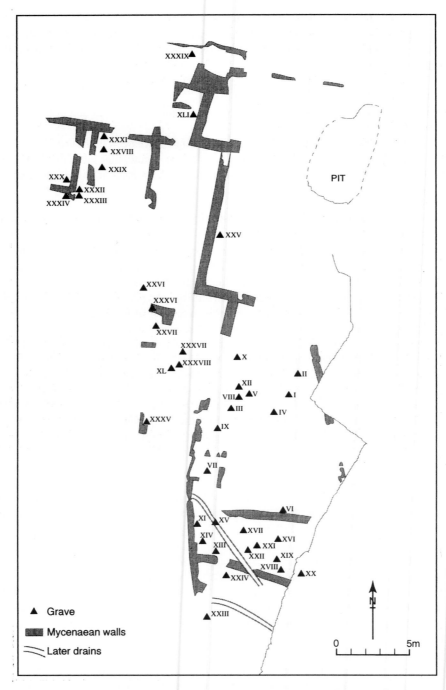

Fig. 4. Area of the Prehistoric Cemetery excavated 1939–53.

14

groups of tholos tombs, see Wace 1949, 16–18). Only sherds of LH I and LH II were found with the MH sherds below the green layer of Plesia clay covering the mound over the tholos (*BSA* 49, 232: see also *BSA* 25, 316; Wace 1949, 39; *BSA* 50, 209; Pélon 1976, 162; Dickinson 1977, 62; French and Iakovides, forthcoming). The dark fill around and under the area of paving slabs in the dromos of the tomb contained only MH (matt-painted) sherds (*PAE* 1955, 218–22).

Museum Site (Fold-out plan; fig. 715–24)
Seven graves of the Prehistoric Cemetery were discovered on the site of the new Museum at Mycenae immediately to the N of the citadel. In the same place there was also a later grave (dated after the early stages of LH IIIC and before the start of Protogeometric) (Onasoglou 1995, 145–6, and parenthetic plate A).

East House (Fold-out plan)
A shaft grave of MH date containing the contracted burial of an adult male was found associated with foundations of MH buildings under the East House excavated by Verdelis in 1963 (*PAE* 1963, 109–10 and pl. 84a).[3] This is the most southerly of the graves of the cemetery.

West House (Fold-out plan)
Two graves of late MH date were discovered under the stone pavement of the court of the West House in hollows in the native rock (Tournavitou 1995, 6; *MT III* 19).

Since the areas excavated represent only a comparatively small area of the Prehistoric Cemetery, and some areas, such as the Ramp House have not been completely excavated to the rock, it is quite likely that the Cemetery contained many more graves, and that graves will continue to be found in future excavations in the area. From time to time virtually complete pots of LH I date (see, for example, *BSA* 71, 103 fig. 15) are found on the lower slopes of the citadel at Mycenae, and these may come from disturbed graves. Around 150 graves or possible graves of the Prehistoric Cemetery have been investigated. This publication deals in detail with 139, of which thirty-three are published here for the first time. Of the remainder, fifty-seven were previously published only in preliminary form.

THE MIDDLE HELLADIC SETTLEMENT

During the period of use of the Prehistoric Cemetery, the hill of Mycenae was already quite densely populated. This is apparent from the remains of MH buildings near the summit, on the west and north sides, and in the north-east corner near the House of the Columns (*AE* 1987, 349). The remains of structures from the MH period are found in all areas of the Prehistoric Cemetery. Inside the later fortification walls, MH walls have been found in the Citadel House Area (*WBM* 1, 40, 41, 45; *AR* 1960–1, 31; 1962–3, 14–15) and a basement of MH date with pithoi containing grain was found in the area east of Tsountas' House (*PAE* 1971, 152).

Outside the later fortifications, an MH hearth pit was found with a series of white clay plaster floors in the area of the Perseia Fountain House where two possible MH graves were also found (*BSA* 48, 24–5). Grave Circle B was found to contain the walls of a series of MH buildings dating from before the construction of the Circle (*GCB* 8–18). A horse-shoe shaped construction of uncertain purpose, but dating to the MH period was found in the southern part of Grave Circle B (*GCB* 124–6). Houses of MH date were destroyed during the construction of the dromos of the Tomb of Aegisthus (*PAE* 1955, 218–22). The remains of a MH house wall were found in the area of the West House in the southern part of the Prehistoric Cemetery (*PAE* 1961, 163–4; *PAE* 1963, 109–10; *MT III* 19–20, 23).

Further away from the Citadel, MH remains have been found on the Kalkani hill (Wace 1949, 21, 42) and on the north end of the Panagia ridge (*BSA* 25, 320; *BSA* 48, 73; *BSA* 59, 244–5; *BSA* 60, 174; *CT* 18, 44), though not as far S as the House of Lead (French and Iakovides, forthcoming). Remains of MH structures have also been found on the SW slope of Ag. Elias (Wace 1949, 47).

Dickinson (1977, 39) interprets these remains as representing a cluster of villages, hamlets, or even isolated houses, rather than a continuously built-up area. The large number of burials of MH date found in the excavated portions of the Prehistoric Cemetery suggest that Mycenae was a populous place in the Middle Bronze Age. Most of the graves investigated contained the burials of children. Until the later stages of the period the graves contained little or nothing apart from the burial: it is not possible to infer very much about the wealth or poverty of the inhabitants of the area at this time. In the later stages of the period new grave types (especially large Shaft Graves) and burial precincts appear. The construction of Grave Circle B in the late stages of MH perhaps marks the separation of élite members of the community from the rest of the population. There is also an increase in the quality and quantity of objects deposited in graves. The wealthiest graves in Grave Circle B date to the final stages of MH. In LH I a new group broke away from this wealthy élite to use a new burial precinct, Grave Circle A, closer to the acropolis, with even more flamboyantly conspicuous grave objects than the wealthiest graves of Grave Circle B. Although Grave Circle B was still in use in LH I, the burials are less wealthy than those of the same date in Grave Circle A, suggesting that the LH I burials in Grave Circle B are of persons of a lower social rank (Graziado 1991, 440). These factors suggest changes (increasing stratification) within society and the emergence of new groups during the later stages of MH.

MH–LH II CEMETERIES AND BURIAL PRACTICES IN THE ARGOLID

THE GENERAL SITUATION

Burial in the Middle Helladic period may be intra-mural or extra-mural. Intra-mural burial is burial within the area of the settlement: the graves are among the houses in the streets and lanes, sometimes close to house walls, like the MH shaft grave close to the wall of a MH house under the East House at Mycenae (*PAE* 1963, 110). Occasionally they are found within a house, under a floor. In the Prehistoric Cemetery East, for example, **PCE'52 Grave XXVIII** was cut through the earliest floor (floor 36) of Middle Helladic House A.[4] The burial in **PCE'52 Grave XXX** was probably interred after floor 26 was laid over wall 3 and over the corridor between walls 2 and 3 in the same area, and perhaps before floor 26 went out of use. **PCE'52 Grave XXVII** was dug after the floor of House B (south of House A in the same area) was laid. **PCE'52 Grave XXVI** may have been dug at about the same time, and also within the house. **PCE'52 Grave XXVII** was re-opened for at least one of its later burials when floor 44, connected with wall 14 (Plan 14) was going out of use. In some cases the house is no longer used at the time the burial is made.[5] Extra-mural burial is burial outside the settlement, whether in isolated graves or in special cemetery areas. The graves in an extra-mural cemetery may be scattered over a wide area. Some extra-mural cemeteries are situated in the countryside at some distance from the settlement, like the MH cemetery at Prosymna (*Prosymna*, 30–50). Grouping has been observed in the arrangement of some of the graves of the Prehistoric Cemetery: **PC'39 Graves I, II and IV** appear to form one group, and **PC'39 Graves III, V, VII, IX, and XII** another (*BSA* 45, 218). Professor Wace expressed the view that the group of child burials found under Room 50 of the House of the Warrior Vase might be a part of the Prehistoric Cemetery reserved for children (*BSA* 50, 191; cf. *DIPG* 34). There is certainly a high preponderance of child burials in the Prehistoric Cemetery, but adult burials are interspersed with them: this inclusion of men, women, and children in the MH cemetery was also observed at Asine (Nordquist 1990, 38).

The decision to create a formal precinct by enclosing an area of the cemetery with a wall appears to be taken when the cemetery has already been in use for some time in the case of an enclosure at Asine which cuts over four cists (*Asine II* 71). Burial precincts may be rectilinear, as at Pefkakia (Caskey 1971, 305), or round, as at Mycenae (on the enclosures of Grave Circles A and B see *MMA* 94–8; *GCB* 18–20 and pl. 6), Malthi (Valmin 1938, 187) and Nichoria (*Hesperia* 44, 73–5). Sometimes only one wall of the burial precinct is discovered, so that its shape and extent remain unknown, as in the North Cemetery at Corinth (*Corinth* XIII, 1–12; see also *Asine II* 71). The Grave Circles at Mycenae form very distinct precincts within the Prehistoric Cemetery for the burials of highly privileged social groups. The excavators of the part of the Prehistoric Cemetery under the Citadel House Area thought that at least some of the MH walls they found there were built to enclose the cemetery area (*WBM* 1, 45). The East–West Wall (see Fold-out plan and *BSA* 50, 203–7 and pls. 36, 39b) has been interpreted as a northern boundary of the area of the Prehistoric Cemetery and the Tomb of Aegisthus. The wall, built of rubble bonded in clay, cuts through the clay cap of the Tomb of Aegisthus, and so postdates the construction of the tholos early in LH IIA. At its western end the lower courses of the East–West wall pass under the foundations of the Great Poros Wall (*BSA* 50, 209–37 and pls. 36, 40–45) built to retain the mound over the Tomb of Clytemnestra, demonstrating that it was built before the construction of the tholos. Before the construction of the Tomb of Clytemnestra the East–West wall may have extended further to the west. A deposit, thought to be votive, was identified at the junction of the East–West wall and the Great Poros Wall (*BSA* 50, 221–2, published in *BSA* 64, 71–93). Lord William Taylour suggested (*BSA* 50, 205) that both the 'votive' deposit and the later burial (*BSA* 50, 214 and pl. 41b) against the Great Poros Wall may indicate that the area was regarded as sacred, and the East–West Wall might have been built to mark out a 'temenos' of graves including the Tomb of Aegisthus and the forty-one graves excavated in the area between 1939 and 1953. The East–West wall cannot be regarded as the northern limit of the Prehistoric Cemetery, because graves were found under the site of the new museum further to the north, and Hood found pits which might have been graves under the Perseia Fountain House (*BSA* 48, 25 and pl. 12), also to the north of the wall. However, it is certainly possible that the East–West Wall marks out an especially important area of the cemetery containing the prestigious Tomb of Aegisthus, rather as Grave Circles A and B mark out the burials of particularly prestigious groups within a cemetery that had already been in use for some time when the wall was constructed.

The cemetery area at some sites may include burial tumuli. In the Argolid there are examples at Argos (Protonariou-Deilaki 1980), Asine, and Dendra (see *Asine II* 70–4 with bibliography). These tumuli are large, circular mounds of earth and stone fill, which may be covered with stones and held in place by a retaining wall (Protonariou-Deilaki 1990b, 94). The earliest tumuli in the Argolid date from MH and burials of many kinds may be made in them over a long period. Tumuli contain pithos burials, cist, shaft, and pit graves from the MH period, but burials in tumuli continue long into the historic period. A tholos tomb is cut into Tumulus C at Dendra (Protonariou-Deilaki 1990b, 92–5), and tumuli sometimes also contain burials of Geometric and Hellenistic date, although it is not very clear whether these later burials are associated with the tumulus by accident or design.

THE MH–LH II CEMETERY AT MYCENAE

Protonariou-Deilaki has advanced the view that the Prehistoric Cemetery at Mycenae was covered by three tumuli dating from the EH period. In her view these tumuli account for the quantities of EH pottery discovered in the area of Grave Circle A. She considers that one tumulus covered the area of Grave Circle A and the Granary, and extended as far as the Citadel House Area: about half of it remains unexcavated (Protonariou-Deilaki 1990b, 85–9). She explains that the tumulus was built up from layers of red earth brought from elsewhere as reported by Tsountas (1893, 100; 1897, 106). Another tumulus covered Grave Circle B, according to her theory, and extended to the east as far as the Great Poros Wall, and to the south as far as the chamber tomb south of Grave Circle B (see Fold-out plan and Protonariou-Deilaki 1990b, 89–91 and 86 fig. 1). This theory rejects the excavators' explanation of the layers of clay covering the mound of the Tomb of Aegisthus as waterproofing to protect the dome, and explains them[6] as the layers of a tumulus.

The discoveries at Argos, Asine, and Dendra of a series of burial tumuli containing graves of the same period as the Shaft Graves at Mycenae (Protonariou-Deilaki 1980; 1990a; 1990b, 94–102; *Asine II*) make the theory of tumuli at Mycenae particularly intriguing, especially considered with the EH III tumulus over the House of the Tiles at Lerna, into which shaft graves were later cut (*Hesperia* 24, 32–4; 25, 155–7 and pl. 43c). However, various scholars argue that the explanation of Hammond, the first scholar in recent years to advance the theory of tumuli at Mycenae,[7] is based on a misunderstanding of the stratigraphical evidence (*GCB* 249–54; Dickinson 1977, 51; *Asine II* 72). Supporters of the theory of three tumuli at Mycenae dating from the EH period must explain (among other difficulties) why so many MH buildings were erected on the tumuli before they reverted, at a later stage of MH, to their original use as tumuli. In my view more evidence would be needed before the theory of three tumuli at Mycenae can be accepted: for the time being it will be wise to regard the Grave Circles at Mycenae as quite exceptional among the MH cemeteries of the Argolid, suggesting the presence of an extraordinary and powerful élite not found elsewhere in the region.

Certainly the Grave Circles at Mycenae appear as the walled burial precincts of a privileged group superimposed on an area which had already been used as a cemetery for a long time. In view of the MH structures found in all parts of the Prehistoric Cemetery, it is difficult to decide whether the burials are intra-mural or extra-mural. Generalization is probably best avoided. The burial near the MH wall under the West House might be intra-mural, but it is not clear whether the building was in use at the time the burial was made. Certainly **PCE'52 Graves XXVIII** and **XXX** appear to have been dug through the floors of a building still in use and **PCE'52 Graves XXVI** and **XXVII** were dug through the floors of another building still in use. As mentioned above, the excavators of the area of the Prehistoric Cemetery under the Citadel House Area suggested that at least some of the MH walls in the Citadel House Area were built to enclose the cemetery area: in my view this might be true of walls **ba** and **pe**. The two pots in a corner at the eastern intersection of walls **id** and **ic** seem to be deliberately placed in a sheltered area suitable for cooking for a funerary ceremony. The urn covered by a 'bunstone' (as described by the excavator, George Huxley) over **PCE'53 Grave XXXVIII** (Pl. 8) was securely wedged against the E face of the central north–south wall in that area, and was evidently intended to be seen against the wall. However, it should also be remembered that some of the MH walls are constructed right over a group of burials as if the builders had no knowledge of the existence of the graves. The bones in Γ **Graves 6, 7, 8, 9,** and **13** were under wall **ic**: those in Γ **Grave 13** underlay wall **id** as well. The bones in Γ **Grave 3** were under wall **ib**.

GRAVE TYPES

The simplest form of grave is the **pit**, which may be cut into earth, or if the earth is too shallow for the full depth of the pit, as often happens at Mycenae, through the earth and into the rock. The floor of a pit grave may be strewn with pebbles. In the case of an earth-cut pit, the excavator may not be aware that s/he is dealing with a grave until the skeleton is found: sometimes s/he finds the sides of the pit, but usually its upper part is lost (Blackburn 1970, 16). These graves are catalogued as unenclosed inhumations.[8] At Mycenae the earth-cut upper part of pits cut through earth and rock may be lost through later building work, which also removes the burial. This leaves a small cutting in the rock which was once the lower part of a grave. Such cuttings are found under the Ramp House and the House of the Warrior Vase.

The pit grave may be large or small. It will be roofed at its mouth, usually with stones or stone slabs. These are often missing, since they are vulnerable to being pulled up by the plough, and to being taken for use in buildings. The cover slabs may rest directly on the rock or hard-packed soil. Alternatively a line of stones may be laid along the edge of the grave to receive them.[9] The cover slabs may be covered with plaster, as in the case of **PCE'52 Grave XXVIII** at Mycenae (Pl. 6*a*). Pit graves are mainly used for individual burials, but they are not infrequently re-opened for later burials. When this happens, the earlier burial may be removed or swept to one side. This practice is discussed further below.

A more elaborate form of pit grave is the **cist**, which occurs in a variety of forms. The word κίστη means a box, as Dickinson points out (1983, 56), and the cists whose walls are formed of four or more large vertical slabs of stone, with further stone slabs used for the roof are certainly extremely box-like. The term cist is also used for a pit lined with walls built in various techniques. A stone-built cist may have dry stone walls constructed from irregular stones, or stones placed horizontally, as in house-walls. (The shaft grave is a later development of this type.) **PC'39 Grave II** is a good example of a cist constructed from large vertical slabs of stone, but its cover slabs were missing at the time of excavation: they might have been pulled up by the plough, or removed in later building. **PC'39 Grave XIII** (Pl. 4*a*) was probably similarly constructed of large vertical slabs of stone, but it had lost not only its cover slabs, but also all the large vertical stones with the exception of that at the N end. Some cists are oval or round, and lined with a ring of stones which may be tilted towards the centre of the ring, like **PCE'52 Grave XXVIII** at Mycenae (Pl. 6) (cf. Grave 78 at Lerna: Blackburn 1970, 76). There are also **brick cists**, which can sometimes be inferred when clay sides are reported, as in **Γ Grave 17** at Mycenae:[10] the sides may be lined with raw clay (*DIPG* 26) or the clay may represent decayed sun-baked bricks. Patches of dark orange or red clay at the mouth of **Γ Grave 17** (Pl. 5*a*) may be an indication of brick roofing.[11] Some MH cists are composite with a slab of stone for one wall, while the other walls are lined with stones or bricks. The inner corner of a disused house may be closed off with a vertical stone and a brick to form a cist. Stone-built and composite cist graves are likely to be roofed with flat stone slabs or smaller stones fitted together. Sometimes a clay coating is applied to the cover slabs in position:[12] the cover slab of **PCE'52 Grave XXVIII** (Pl. 6*a*) was covered with white plaster, and **PCE'52 Grave XXVI** had a layer of waterproof Plesia clay on top of the grave fill.

Most cists and pits are small, and small graves of these types continue to be constructed and used right through the Mycenaean period. However, in certain cases larger pits and cists were required, and the roofing of these, particularly where large stone slabs were used, must have been a challenge. If the grave was to be re-used, the stone slabs of the roof had to be removed and replaced, and the effort required to manoeuvre these very large slabs of stone may have been a factor leading to the development of the Shaft Grave.

The Shaft Grave is a more elaborate type of pit grave, with the difference that the roof is not at the mouth of the grave, but some way below it, leaving a 'shaft' between the roof of the grave and the surface. The floor of a shaft grave tends to be strewn with pebbles, as in the case of pits and cists. The roof, however, is supported on wooden beams laid across the grave: these may be supported on a shelf cut in the rock, or on a wall of horizontally-placed stones lining the sides of the grave. The roofing material may be brushwood or in more ambitious constructions, slabs of stone, and the whole roof is sealed with a layer of waterproof clay. As long as the roof beams remain sound, the roof takes the weight of the soil filling the shaft, and the burial and objects deposited with it are protected from contact with the grave fill. The shaft above the grave is filled

20

in with earth, and the grave marked at the surface, perhaps with a pile of stones,[13] or a grave stele.[14] If the grave is to be re-used, the shaft must be opened and the roof broken. The roofing material of a shaft grave is more easily removed and replaced than the huge slabs of stone used to cover the larger pits and cists, but the effort required to empty the shaft and reopen the roof is still very considerable.

Sometimes a burial is found in a broken **jar** or pithos. It is unlikely that broken jars were kept against the possibility that children in the family would die, and it is more likely that the jars had to be broken so that the burial could be fitted into them. The practice of breaking a jar to accommodate a burial is found in the West Cemetery at Eleusis, where a large amphora originally used as a grave-marker, the magnificent Middle Proto-Attic amphora by the Polyphemus painter, was used to contain the burial of a child. The lower half of the vessel was sawn off, the child's body was placed inside, and the lower portion of the vessel was clamped back together with lead (Morris 1984, 11). In the case of MH jar burials, the jar is usually closed with another broken vessel, whose base is left projecting from the mouth of the jar. The jar containing the burial might be deposited directly in the soil, or it might be placed in a pit or cist grave.[15] Jar burials are most often used to contain the remains of only one individual, usually an infant, but examples are known from Asine and Argos of the burial of two or more adults in jar burials.[16] Γ **Grave 1** at Mycenae may be an example of a jar burial for an infant.

As a rule, burials are made singly. However, it is sometimes clear that two burials were made at the same time, as for example the woman and baby in Γ **Grave 13** at Mycenae, or 1972–5 at Asine, which contained the skeleton of an infant with a 30 year-old woman (*Asine II* 25–6).

RE-USE

In many cases at Mycenae and elsewhere, a skull or a few bones are found, sometimes with grave offerings, but the remains are clearly not *in situ* and no grave can be found associated with the burial.[17] Such burials have been removed from their graves either accidentally, because the grave was disturbed in the course of later agricultural or building work, or deliberately, because the burial was removed from its resting-place to make way for a later burial in the grave. In the latter case, the earlier interments may be found in the fill of the grave, because they have been thrown into the soil shovelled out when the grave was re-opened, and shovelled back into the grave when the fill was replaced after the later burial (Dietz 1991, 106). Cases of re-use virtually require the removal of the earlier burial from small graves, because there is otherwise no room for any more bodies, but as graves become larger, there are two alternative methods of dealing with the earlier burials in a grave. They may either be shovelled out, as before, so that they are found in the fill or further afield, or they may be swept to one side, so that the bones are found partially articulated at the side of the grave, or in a heap in a corner, together with such grave objects as are not removed at the later funeral. Earlier burials were found swept aside. In 1952 and 1953 deposits thought to be from graves were found in the Prehistoric Cemetery outside the fortification walls at Mycenae. If this material had been removed from graves, they might have been destroyed during construction of the mound over the Tomb of Aegisthus. I wish to emphasize that we are not really in a position to infer that this practice of removing earlier burials or sweeping them to one side indicates a lack of respect for the dead (as suggested by Blackburn 1970, 6–7). It is clear, however, that no importance was attached to their resting permanently undisturbed after

PLATE 4

(a)

(b)

(a) **PC'39 Graves XI, XV, XIII and XIV** cut in bed rock; (b) **PC'39 Grave XI**, slab lined cist.

PLATE 5

(*a*)

(*b*)

(*a*) **Γ Grave 17**, brick lined cist, from above; (*b*) **PC'39 Grave III**: rock cut shaft with pottery *in situ*.

(*a*)

(*b*)

(*a*) **PCE'52 Grave XXVIII**: circular stone lined pit, with cover slab; (*b*) **PCE'52 Grave XXVIII**, with cover slab removed to show tightly contracted burial.

burial. The living community needs to be protected from risks associated with the process of decomposition, whereas bones do not constitute a significant risk to the health of the living. Whether the individual was identified with the body, but thought to be absent from the bare bones, is best left in the realm of conjecture. Dismantling graves in a ceremony amounting to a second funeral may be part of the process of constructing memory and forgetting the individual (see Cavanagh 1978; *DIPG*: second burial). The animal bones found with the graves of the Prehistoric Cemetery at Mycenae and in other cemeteries of similar date may be taken as evidence of mortuary feasting. The graves themselves contain vessels for the consumption of food and drink. The Prehistoric Cemetery contains spaces enclosed by walls where vessels for eating and especially drinking have been found. It has always been usual to interpret these vessels as the receptacles of offerings to the dead. However, they may be the equipment of mortuary ceremonies carried out by the community, with eating, drinking, dancing, and perhaps the consumption of narcotics, in an attempt to tame the memory of the dead (see Hamilakis 1998, 116–22).

GRAVE MARKERS

It is perhaps not unreasonable to suppose that a grave would be used and re-used by the members of a single family, who would have to mark it in some way so that the grave could be tended, and re-opened, if required, for later burials. MH–LH II **grave markers** take various forms. Sometimes a pile of stones is heaped over the grave, as Grave 1971–3 at Asine was covered with a layer of large stones (the size of human heads) embedded in moist clay (*Asine II* 36). According to Keramopoullos (1918, 58), the graves in Grave Circle A were all marked by heaped earth and stones: in Grave Circle B, Graves Ξ, Σ, and possibly Ξ-1 were also marked by a heap of stones (Mylonas 1973, 177, 185, 226). These stone piles may indicate status (Dickinson 1977, 42). The edges of the grave may be delineated at the surface by a line of stones,[18] like the graduated line of stones associated with **Γ Grave 15** at Mycenae. Lerna Grave 167 had three huge stones in a row at the surface (Blackburn 1970, 133). A pottery vessel may be used to mark the grave, like the skyphos used to mark Tumulus Γ grave 70 at Argos (Protonariou-Deilaki 1980, 72 and pl. Γ51, 4 and 7). **PCE'53 Grave XXXVIII** at Mycenae was re-used: it was marked by an urn covered with a flat circular stone (Pl. 8). The urn was securely wedged against the main North–South wall in the area. A large stone may be used to mark a grave, like the small slab marking Grave 136 at Lerna (Blackburn 1970, 116). A large and very heavy stone, possibly ironstone, which might have been a grave marker was found in the fill of **PC'39 Grave III**. A stele, like the stelai in the two Grave Circles at Mycenae is a more elaborate form of grave marker. Grave stelai are not restricted to the Grave Circles at Mycenae: they are found at Lerna, for example, and Argos.[19] All the forms of grave-marker mentioned so far are durable, but more perishable materials, such as wood, may also have been used. The position of **PCE'52 Grave XXVI** would have been apparent even after it was filled in: three upright slabs laid in a row on the eastern side of the grave projected above the green Plesia clay sealing the fill of the grave.

As well as the deliberate re-use of graves, there is a tendency to go on digging further graves in more or less the same spot, so that a later grave breaks in upon one or more earlier graves, as **Γ Grave 6** breaks in upon **Γ Grave 13** (Pl. 7*b*).[20] This practice is probably to be explained by a combination of factors: a grave marker might have been removed, for example, or the existence of the grave and its occupant forgotten.[21] Since the area of soft rock occupied by the Prehistoric Cemetery is the closest to the acropolis suitable for cutting graves, it is not surprising that later generations who knew little of the older graves continued to find it a convenient cemetery.

BURIAL CUSTOMS

The method of burial is inhumation. There are no signs of burning on human bones which would indicate cremation in MH–LH II contexts. Graves are generally too small to accommodate adult burials at full length, and this means that most burials are found in a contracted position. Burials tend to lie on one side, sometimes on their backs, with the head pointing in no particular direction, and the legs bent at the knees, and sometimes drawn up against the body. The contracted position may be explained by the small size of the majority of graves: it is quite likely that bodies were tied in a contracted position to make them easier to fit into the small grave pits. If such a custom was usual, its persistence would help to explain the contracted position of some burials in larger graves such as **PC'39 Grave X**, where an extended burial could have been accommodated. Occasionally, as in **PCE'52 Grave XXV**, the skeleton lay contracted on its front with the head tilted to one side (Pl. 7a). The burials of infants may be extended or contracted. As graves become larger, the extended position is possible, and burials in the later shaft graves at Mycenae were found in the extended position, as seen in Grave Γ of Grave Circle B (*GCB* 44 fig. 5).

In **Γ Grave 15** at Mycenae, the skeleton lay against a slab of rock which might perhaps be regarded as a kind of stone 'pillow': certainly 'pillows' have been observed in Early Cycladic cemeteries[22] and paralleled in mainland cemeteries such as Agios Kosmas (Mylonas 1959, 83, 117–8). Stone pillows are also found in MH graves at Asine (Nordquist 1987, 94–5). In Grave Circle B a heap of sand and small stone forming a kind of pillow was found under the head of the skeleton in Grave I.[23]

GRAVE OFFERINGS AND ASSOCIATED FINDS

The objects found in graves may be divided into two categories. The first would more properly be called 'grave offerings' since they were placed deliberately in the grave at the time the burial took place, although they might later be removed from their original position when the grave was re-used or otherwise disturbed. The second category should be thought of as 'associated finds': these are items, usually sherds and fragments of obsidian blades, that are in the grave by chance. They may already have been lying in the soil at the time the grave was cut, or they may have fallen into the hole as the grave was opened or refilled. The majority of MH graves contain no grave objects. Where they occur, the most common 'grave offerings' are pots, especially cups and jugs. A cup may be directly in front of the face of the skeleton, as in **PCE'52 Grave XXV** at Mycenae (Pl. 7a), or near the head or hands.[24] Unfortunately, we generally do not know what was in the pots. Traces of oil and flour were found in some of the pots in Grave Circle B (Grave I: *MMA* 100; *GCB* 113 (I-97), 114 (I-98)), suggesting that the dead were thought to be in need of foodstuffs. One is reminded of Antigone in her underground tomb (Sophocles, *Antigone* 775).

PLATE 7

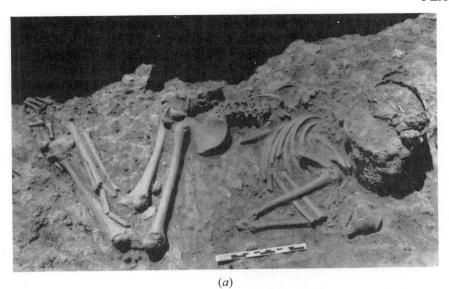

(*a*)

(*b*)

(*a*) **PCE'52 Grave XXV**: unenclosed inhumation contracted on left side with stone vase *in situ*;
(*b*) **Γ Grave 6**: unenclosed inhumation contracted on right side: above tightly contracted earlier
Grave 13. From S.

PLATE 8

(*a*)

(*b*)

(*a*) **PCES1'53 Grave XXXVIII**: circular stone marker *in situ*; (*b*) **PCES1'53 Grave XXXVIII**: re-use, showing two skulls and circular stone marker.

28

Jewellery, where it occurs as a grave offering, may be an isolated bead, or a few beads of stone, bone, or vitreous materials. In the graves of women and girls a clay 'spindle whorl' is not an unusual find. Protonariou-Deilaki argues that these would be more correctly interpreted as the decorative head of a dress pin made of wood, bone, or bronze (Protonariou-Deilaki 1990*a*, 75 fig. 10). In a number of graves at Lerna a terracotta whorl was found near the shoulder of a female burial[25] suggesting Mrs Protonariou-Deilaki's interpretation is correct, and that, as she suggests (Protonariou-Deilaki 1990*a*, 79), the dead were fully dressed at the time of burial. Smaller examples could also have been beads.

The animal bones sometimes found on top of the covering of the grave, perhaps some way below the surface, and sometimes in the grave fill, suggest that when the grave was closed a funerary meal might be cooked over it and consumed by mourners. This impression is strengthened by the cooking pots, drinking vessels, and other containers for liquids (jugs, amphorae) associated with the graves.

THE GRAVES OF THE CITADEL HOUSE AREA (GROUP Γ)

The stages represented by the ceramic record in the Citadel House Area at Mycenae are set out in *WBM* 1, 7–9, and 12–13 (in the Diagram of the History of the Site). Here we shall be concerned with Phase IV, the late MH–LH IIB period, represented by a number of pit and cist graves cut into the lowest levels and into the bedrock. There are several small walls of MH date in the area: of which some may mark the limits of the cemetery area. The terrace wall, **mj**, **ai**, **zj** supporting the LH IIIB buildings may well be of the same date.

Burials were found at nineteen locations under the Citadel House Area. Some of these locations were the site of more than one burial. Each of these locations has been numbered as a grave, although in one or two cases the burial was scattered and nothing which could be described as a grave was found. In these cases the burial may well have been removed from its original resting-place to make room for a later burial. In addition, the two large pots, 69-501 and 69-502, found next to wall **pe** on the west side might have been used for burials. Some of the graves have been disturbed by the construction of later walls or graves. The excavators named most of these burials by letters: burials A–J for the burials found in 1968 in Γ21/22; the letters A–C were used again for the three burials found in Γ23 in the same year. No letters or numbers were allocated to the burials found in Γ21 and Γ31 in 1966. Since the letters A–C were used in 1968 for both the burials found in Γ23 and also for three of those found in Γ21/22, confusion is avoided in this publication by the use of the consecutive Arabic numerals 1–19 to number all the graves in the Citadel House Area (see individual grave entries below, and Fig. 5).

In addition to the Arabic numeral assigned to each grave, the catalogue also gives the letter allocated to a burial by the excavators. Some burials were not designated by any letter. Full details of each grave are given in the fiche: a brief discussion and interpretation of each grave is given here, and the findings compared with what is known of other graves in the Prehistoric Cemetery at Mycenae, and other cemeteries of similar date.

Γ Grave 1 (Γ21 1966) (Fig. 3; fiche 221–4)
A wheelmade pottery jar of coarse, gritty clay with a reddish-buff slip burnished on the outside found next to the MH wall **jx** was thought to have perhaps contained a burial, although it must be emphasised that no bones were found in the jar.

Γ Grave 2 (Γ21 1966) (Figs. 3 and 5; fiche 225–7)
Grave 2 is described as a 'small cutting in the rock': it may well have been closed with cover slabs at the time of its construction. It had contained the burial of a child, although only a few bones survived at the time of excavation. A warped tripod cauldron (68-408) found west of wall **ib** may be associated with this grave.

Γ Grave 3 (Γ21 1966 and 1968) (Figs. 3 and 5; fiche 228–9)
A cutting (called a 'bothros' by the excavator) under wall **ib** was interpreted as a possible grave (**Grave 3a**), although no bones were found in it. At the bottom of the bothros-pit was **Grave 3b**, a 'small cutting with cover slab'. This grave is not a built cist in Dickinson's (1983, 56–7) sense of the term: it is a pit cut into the rock and roofed with a slab. The slab may be seen in place in the bothros, fiche 229: 3061. The burial in this grave was that of a male infant up to one month old. The grave fill was very loose soft rich brown soil. It is unlikely that this grave was disturbed.

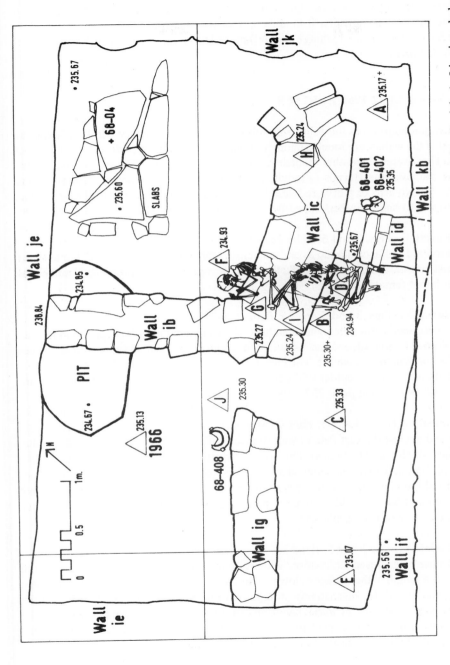

Fig. 5.   Graves below area 36 of the Citadel House Area. A list of the Arabic numerals assigned to Burials A–J is given below.

Γ21/22'68	Burial A	Burial E	Γ Grave 11
Γ21/22'68	Burial B	Burial F	Γ Grave 6
Γ21/22'68	Burial C	Burial G	Γ Grave 7
Γ21/22'68	Burial D		

Γ21/22'68	Burial H	Γ Grave 9
Γ21/22'68	Burial I	Γ Grave 8
Γ21/22'68	Burial J	Γ Grave 5

Γ21/22'68	Burial A	Γ Grave 14
Γ21/22'68	Burial B	Γ Grave 12
Γ21/22'68	Burial C	Γ Grave 10
Γ21/22'68	Burial D	Γ Grave 13

Γ Grave 4 (Γ21/22 1968) (Figs. 3 and 5; fiche 230–1)

This grave was a small pit with cover slabs which fitted together like a mosaic. No bones were found in the grave, which is very small. Given the tendency of the bones of the very young and the very old to dissolve completely, it is unlikely that the grave was disturbed. It probably contained the burial of an infant or young child. A flattened bronze cylinder seal (68-04) (Pl. 14*c*) was found in the grave.

Γ GRAVES 5–14 (Γ21/22 1968 BURIALS A–J)

The excavation notebook gives the following information in the summary: 'In Γ22 Trench C below the level of the walls were found a number of burials: one adult, one adolescent, and about seven infants. They were lying either on bedrock, or shortly above it… The infant burials were found all over the area, but Burials D (adult, **Grave 13**) and F (adolescent, **Grave 6**) were associated (Pl. 7*b*). No cists or pits were found for the burials. They seem to be all MH.' In fact Burial F (**Γ Grave 6**) had disturbed the earlier Burial D (**Γ Grave 13**).

Γ Grave 5 (Burial J) (Figs. 3 and 5; fiche 232–3)

Grave 5 is described in the catalogue as an 'unenclosed inhumation'. It was found in a corner between the east face of wall **ig** and the baulk: the burial was partly inside the baulk. The skeleton was that of an infant female, *164 Myc.*

Γ Grave 6 (Burial F) (Figs. 3 and 5; Pl. 7*b*; fiche 234–7)

Grave 6 is also described in the catalogue as an 'unenclosed inhumation'. It lay partly under wall **ic**, and had disturbed **Grave 13**, another 'unenclosed inhumation'. Both graves could have been damaged by the construction of wall **ic**. The burial, an adolescent female of about 13 years (*160 Myc.*) lay with its feet on the shoulder of the burial in **Grave 13**; its legs had disturbed the ribs of the burial in **Grave 13**: see fiche 237: 3093.

Γ Grave 7 (Burial G) (Figs. 3 and 5; fiche 238)

Below wall **ic** and against the east face of wall **ib** pieces of a child's skull were found together with a few bones which might be human. This was called Burial G. No sherds were found in the direct area of this burial, which is catalogued as an 'unenclosed inhumation,' although the bones were scattered and found together with bones from *162 Myc.* in **Grave 9** and fragments of adult skeletons and animal bones. It is likely that by the time of excavation all these bones had been moved from their original resting-places.[26]

Γ Grave 8 (Burial I) (Figs. 3 and 5; fiche 239)

Burial I was another 'unenclosed inhumation' which also underlies wall **ic**: it was found scattered over the whole N–S length of the surface below wall **ic**. It could have come from a grave damaged by the construction of wall **ic**: alternatively, it might have been thrown out and scattered when its grave was re-used. Certainly the burial had been disturbed from its original position, and the location of its grave is unknown. A speck of charcoal found in the area of this burial might come from the cooking of a funerary meal.

Γ Grave 9 (Burial H) (Figs. 3 and 5; fiche 240)

Catalogued as an unenclosed inhumation, this fragmentary infant burial (*162 Myc.*) was found with another fragmentary infant burial (*161 Myc.* in **Grave 7**) scattered below wall **ic**. Fragments of adult skeletons and animal bones were found with them (see p. 21). All this material is likely to have been removed from a grave or graves either deliberately to make way for further burials or accidentally when walls were built.

Γ Grave 10 (Burial C) (Figs. 3 and 5; fiche 241–2)

This unenclosed inhumation burial of an infant had a grave fill of loose dark brown soil containing small stones. An obsidian blade is an associated find, unlikely to be connected with the burial.

Γ Grave 11 (Burial E) (Figs. 3 and 5; fiche 243–6)

The bones of this unenclosed inhumation were found with two gold discs and the lower part of an MH goblet under a large, flat stone. The bones did not lie in their original position, and might have been disturbed by fallen stones east of wall **ic**. An obsidian chip is an associated find.

Γ Grave 12 (Burial B) (Figs. 3 and 5; fiche 247–8)

The exact position and form of **Grave 12** is unknown since the bones were only later separated from sheep bones (during the preliminary bone study), perhaps from a funerary meal, found to the west of wall **id** (see p. 21).

Γ Grave 13 (Burial D) (Figs. 3 and 5; fiche 249–53)

The heavily contracted burial of an adult woman (*158 Myc.*) underlay walls **id** and **ic**. With her were the bones of a small infant (*157 Myc.*). The burial was unenclosed, and had been disturbed by the burial in **Γ Grave 6** (Pl. 7*b*). An obsidian flake and part of an obsidian blade are associated finds.

Γ Grave 14 (Burial A) (Figs. 3 and 5; fiche 254–60)

Numerous animal bones were found in loose brown soil containing numerous small stones east of wall **id**. The bones of an infant were separated from these animal bones. The location of this burial and the type of grave used are therefore unknown.

Perhaps associated with this burial are two pots, 68-401 and 68-402 (Pls. 9, 10*a–c*), erroneously marked as graves on *WBM* 1 plan 7. One of these, 68-401 is a small tripod cooking pot with signs of burning. The other, 68-402, is an LH IIA four-handled pottery jar with an ancient break, suggesting it might have been moved in antiquity from its position. I would tentatively suggest that the animal bones are the remains of the funerary meal which became confused with Burial A when the latter was moved from its original position to make way for a later burial. Burial A then became part of the grave fill together with the animal bones. The vessels may have been removed with Burial A from a grave. The concrete-like deposit on them is a mystery. A similar deposit is found on a group of sixth-century BC vases in Belfast, the McElderry collection, which is known to have come from tombs in Boiotia. It is possible, therefore, that these vases were once in a roofed grave into which water carried fine particles of soil containing chemicals which then dried and hardened, gradually building up the deposit on the pots.

Γ Grave 15 (Γ31 1966) (Fig. 3; fiche 261–5)
Under wall **gc** the heavily contracted burial of an adult female was found lying partly on a slab (a pillow?) by a piece of rock. By the time the burial was found, it was no longer possible to tell if the bedrock had been cut to form a cist. A graduated line of stones (medium in the north, becoming smaller towards the south) under wall **gc** might perhaps mark the position of the grave.[27] The only item deliberately placed with the burial was a terracotta 'spindle whorl' (probably the head of a dress pin of perishable material (Protonariou-Deilaki 1990a, 75 fig. 10 and 79)). The two fragments of a jar are probably associated finds.

Γ Grave 16 (Γ23 1968 Burial B) (Fig. 3; fiche 266–7)
This grave, catalogued as an earth-cut inhumation with cover slabs is probably classifiable in Dickinson's terms as an earth-cut pit with cover slabs. Under the slabs was grave fill of soft, dark, loose soil: the contracted burial of an infant in fragmentary condition lay on bedrock. The burial is unlikely to have been disturbed.

Γ Grave 17 (Γ23 1968 Burial C) (Fig. 3; Pl. 5a; fiche 268–70)
This earth-cut pit grave is probably a brick-lined cist.[28] It contained the burial of an infant thought by Angel to be premature. The patch of dark orange stony soil may perhaps be the decayed remains of a mud brick roof.[29] The blackened upper surface of this orange patch may be the mark of fire from a funerary meal on the mud brick roof after the grave was closed. The south wall consisted of a block of dark red pebbly earth, very hard. The earth at the east side was harder than the fill and entirely dark brown. The west wall too was harder than the fill, and entirely red. There was a block of orange earth on the west side of the grave, with dark earth again to the west of it. The earth sides of the pit sound like the remains of a lining of raw clay or sun-baked brick, long since decayed. The blackened stone on the south side of the grave may represent a grave-marker.

Γ Grave 18 (ΓMBW 1968) (Fig. 3; fiche 271–5)
This rock-cut pit grave, probably of LH III date, partly underlay wall **av** of the LH IIIB Temple building (*WBM* 10, 11 and figs. 2–3). It had been used repeatedly for burials and their order was impossible to determine. A fragmentary LH IIIA1 terracotta figurine (68-59) and sherds of an LH IIIA1 goblet (68-442) were found in Level I with the last burial, that of an infant. The remains of an earlier, disturbed infant burial (bones, a tooth, and fragments of skull) were also found in Level I, with a femur fragment of a third individual. At the bottom of the grave, three *femora* projected from stones under wall **av**.

69-501, 69-502 (Fig. 3; fiche 278–80)
Two large storage pots, 69-501 and 69-502 were found lying next to wall **pe** and partly underneath wall **pd**. The two vessels rested on an unusually smooth black rounded stone. It is possible that the pots were used as containers for burials which have decayed completely.

There were probably other graves in the Citadel House Area: unexcavated burials are likely to remain under the LH III walls, and more graves may well have been destroyed by later buildings.

PLATE 9

Γ22 Trench C. Two pots (68-401, 68-402) *in situ*, possibly associated with burial A (Γ **Grave 14**), amongst ?remains of funerary meal.

PLATE 10

(a)

(b)

(c)

(*a*) 68-401 small tripod cooking vessel; (*b*) 68-402 LH II four-handled jar; (*c*) **PCE'52 Grave XXIX** MH juglet, 52-602.

PLATE 11

(*a*)

(*b*)

(*a*) **PC SE'50 Grave XXIII** MH pottery: 50-276 piriform bowl (*right*); 50-277 dipper with loop handle (*left*); (*b*) **PC SE'50 Grave XXIII**: 50-275 MH jug.

PLATE 12

(*a*)

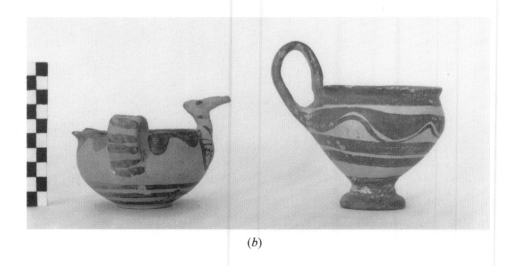

(*b*)

(*a*) South House: dish from MH grave below East Room; (*b*) **PC'39 Grave III**, LH I pottery: 39-236 cup with plastic duck's head (*left*); 39-237 goblet (*right*).

PLATE 13

(*a*)

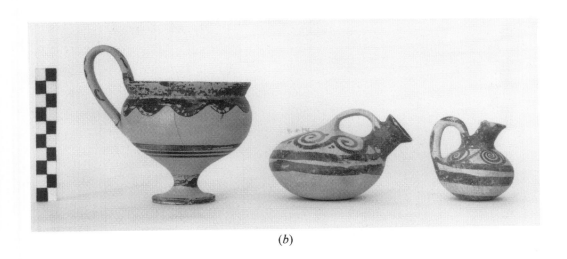

(*b*)

(*a*) **PC'39 Grave III**, LH I pottery: 39-240 LH I–II feeding bowl (*left*); 39-241 goblet (*right*);
(*b*) **PC'39 Grave III**, LH I pottery: 39-239 goblet with one high-swung handle (*left*); 39-238
askos with loop handle (*centre*); 39-242 small jug with cutaway neck and loop handle (*right*).

PLATE 14

(a)

(b)

(c)

(a) **PC'39 Grave VIII**: 39-540 gold beads; 39-541 decayed amber beads; (b) **PCE'52 Grave XXV**, 52-624 serpentine vase; (c) **Γ Grave 4**: 68-04 bronze seal.

THE HUMAN REMAINS (fiche 725)

The late J. Lawrence Angel, Curator of Physical Anthropology at the Smithsonian Institution was the physical anthropologist most closely acquainted with the Bronze Age skeletal material from the Argolid. His methods for judging the age of skeletons at death are explained in his study of the material from Lerna (Angel 1971, 69–71 and *GCB* i. 384). For non-adult skeletons, he uses the degree of ossification and closure of epiphyses, and the stage of eruption of the teeth. For adults he uses the phase of the pubic symphyseal face, the degree of closure of sutures of the skull, the appearance of exostoses at sites of tendon attachment, and the development of atrophy and shrinkage in spongy and compact bone. Angel's results should be treated with caution, however, in the light of the findings of the Spitalfields project. The vaults at Christchurch, Spitalfields, in London yielded 983 interments, mainly in coffins. Plates giving name, age, and date of death were attached to 387 of the coffins, which were deposited between 1729 and 1857. The vaults were sealed in 1867. The skeletons from Spitalfields were aged according to the Complex method of Acsàdi and Nemeskéri (Acsàdi and Nemeskéri 1970).[30] Comparison between the ages of the subjects from Spitalfields as determined by the Complex Method and their real ages revealed a systematic error which resulted in those under 40 being over-aged and those over 70 being under-aged. Less than 30% of the Spitalfields sample were correctly aged by the Complex Method (Molleson and Cox 1993, 167–9, 214–15).

Angel (*GCB* i. 379–97) gives a brief report on a study he made in 1937 of six males from Grave Circle A from the 1876 excavations of Schliemann and the 1877 excavations of Stamatakes. Later, in the summer of 1954, he studied 94 Mycenaeans. Of these, 16 men, 5 women, and 2 children were from Grave Circle B, excavated and studied between the end of 1951 and the summer of 1954 by Professor Mylonas and Dr. Papademetriou. Thirty-six of the skeletons studied in 1954 came from graves found in the Helleno-British excavations of 1939, 1952, and 1953 by Professor Wace in the area of the Prehistoric Cemetery. The remaining skeletons studied by Angel in 1954 came from excavations in the Cyclopaean Terrace Building and other locations at Mycenae and a few came from later graves found in the area of the Prehistoric Cemetery. The skeletal evidence suggested the subjects from Grave Circle B enjoyed strikingly good health: they were taller and more massive than the rest of the population, with large hands and feet and pronounced markings on the skeleton for muscle attachments. The lines of arrested growth in the enamel of the teeth common at Lerna and other Middle Bronze Age sites are not found in the skeletons from the Grave Circles, suggesting good diet in childhood and adolescence, and no periods of partial starvation such as the general population must have experienced. The comparative freedom from dental disease among the subjects from the Grave Circles adds to the picture of excellent health. Nevertheless Angel calculates the average age at death for the subjects studied from the Grave Circles at thirty-six, no greater than that of the average population at the time. Angel associates this unexpectedly short average lifespan with the evidence of trauma displayed by the skeletal remains, suggesting that the males were indeed fighters and champions. He might have referred to Sarpedon's νεῖκος to Glaucus (*Il.* 12. 310–28) which presents a similar picture of kings who enjoy the best of everything at the price of defending their communities in times of need.

Facial reconstructions of subjects from Grave Circle B found certain physical resemblances between some of the burials. The remains in Grave Circle A were considered too fragmentary for reconstruction to be attempted (Prag *et al.* 1995).

From the graves of the Prehistoric Cemetery excavated in 1952, Angel examined seventeen skeletons, mostly those of infants (including foetuses). One skeleton was found to have died at the age of eight, and two at fourteen: no mature adults were studied. From the graves excavated in 1953, Angel again examined seventeen skeletons, eight of which belonged to infants or foetuses who had died before their first birthday: four died before reaching the age of five, two between the ages of five and twelve, and only two were the burials of mature adults. From the eighteen graves excavated in the Citadel House Area, Angel studied remains from sixteen or seventeen skeletons in 1972. Of these, the only adults were two (possibly three) women.[31] These women were estimated to be in their forties when they died. *148 Myc.* had suffered a fracture of the neck of the femur, unhealed at the time of death. *158 Myc.* (Burial D) was thought by Angel to have borne 7–11 children.[32] *160 Myc.* was a female of about 13 years. The remainder of the burials were those of infants, mostly new-born, and two not carried to full term. The number of children's graves in the cemetery suggest that the rate of infant mortality was high, as it was at Lerna, and as is usual 'in all human populations before the recent industrial and atomic revolutions'(Angel 1971, 71). Angel suggests that of an average of five children born to every woman in the community at Lerna, three would die, and the figures at Mycenae seem not incompatible with this possibility. It is not really possible to go further and speculate on the size of the community which made use of the Prehistoric Cemetery. Additional cemeteries must have been used, and perhaps these contained a higher proportion of adult burials, but they must have been further from the acropolis (cf. *Keos VII*, 184).

In relation to the number of graves so far found in the Prehistoric Cemetery, the subjects examined by Angel are too few to permit more detailed conclusions. Angel studied the remains of 234 people from Lerna IV, V, and VI and described his sample as 'laughably small' (Angel 1971, 69) as a basis for discussion of Lerna's social biology and ecology. Apart from the graves enclosed in the two Grave Circles, ninety-five graves and fifteen possible graves have been investigated in the Prehistoric Cemetery. In nineteen of these, the burials were completely missing, and in a few others the remains of any burials were only fragmentary. Given that the bones of those who died in extreme old age and in infancy survive poorly, and in the ground the bones of females survive less well than those of males (Angel 1971, 71; Coleman 1977, 134), we should not be surprised to find graves in which the burial is missing or incomplete.

CONCLUSIONS

For most of the long MH period, the cemetery at Mycenae is not very different from the cemeteries at the neighbouring sites of Corinth, Prosymna, and Lerna. Although the existence of tumuli at Mycenae remains hypothetical, the graves of the Prehistoric Cemetery also resemble those found in the tumuli at Asine and Argos. The picture which emerges from the MH graves of the Prehistoric Cemetery is one of extreme simplicity: the graves are very small and simple, and nothing is deposited with many of the burials. Where they do occur, grave objects are restricted to dress fastenings of no value, or perhaps a pottery vessel, usually a cup. Infant mortality is high, life expectancy short, and women may bear large numbers of children, many of whom die in infancy.

Towards the end of MH, small shaft graves like **C* 1955 Shaft Grave** begin to appear and small items of jewellery are deposited with burials, like the carnelian bead in **PC'39 Grave IX** and the gold discs in **Γ Grave 11**. Instead of just one pottery vessel, there may be several, as in **Γ Grave 2**. Grave Circle B is established in an area of disused buildings and graves. The earliest graves in Circle B are not unlike graves of similar date elsewhere in the Prehistoric Cemetery: they are small in size, with few grave objects. The earliest burials in Grave Circle A also resemble graves in the Prehistoric Cemetery, and probably antedate the original construction of the circle. Both Grave Circles appear to be in simultaneous use in the later stages of MH. The later graves in Grave Circle A (I, III, IV, and V) are extremely large and contain an extraordinary wealth of grave objects. They are quite unlike any of the other graves in the Prehistoric Cemetery.

Burials continue to be made in the Prehistoric Cemetery during LH I–II: **PC'39 Grave III** (Pl. 5*b*) is a rock-cut pit of LH I date, with plentiful pottery (Pls. 12*b*, 13), gold ornaments, and beads. LH II pottery is plentiful in **PC'39 Grave VIII**, which also contains gold and amber beads (Pl. 14*a*). **Γ Grave 4** contained a seal of LH I–II date (Pl. 14*c*). Large deposits of LH I–II material, including ivory inlays and other objects of value thought to have been cleared from graves were discovered in 1952 and 1953. The Prehistoric Cemetery may therefore have been more heavily used at this time than is apparent from the surviving graves. At this date a decline might have been expected in the use of the Prehistoric Cemetery, because new tholos tombs and chamber tomb cemeteries were becoming established to the west.

Burials of LH IIIA date in the Prehistoric Cemetery, like **Γ Grave 18** in the Citadel House Area, are unusual. Interest in the area as a cemetery appears to revive at the end of the Mycenaean period with LH IIIC burials like **PCE'53 Grave XXXIX** and the late burial under the new museum (**Museum Grave 1**: Onasoglou 1995, 145–6). Burials of Submycenaean, Protogeometric, Geometric, and Hellenistic date are also found there (*BSA* 49, 259–66; *BSA* 50, 239–47, *BSA* 48, 9).

43

ENDNOTES

1 Schliemann 1878, 162ff. There are only four vases (Karo 1930–33, 16, 63, nos. 157–60). In the National Museum at Athens there are two other unbroken Middle Helladic vases from Schliemann's excavations (nos. 1110 and 1305) which may well have come from MH graves; Wace 1949, 61, n. 5.

2 This grave is not shown on the Fold-out plan. The grave was about 1.75 m long, 0.84 m wide, and 0.73 m deep. Its direction is from N to S. In late Mycenaean times the pit was cut at its W side by another pit and the whole shaft was used as a rubbish pit. The grave itself was completely robbed and in the rubbish pit much pottery from the LH IIIB–C period was found. This information comes from handwritten notes sent to Wace by Dr. Papademetriou.

3 The head was to N and the trunk leaned slightly to the left.

4 See Plan 14: walls 1, 2, 3 and 6 seem part of the original plan of the house.

5 At Asine, for example, graves often seem to be in areas used as waste land at the time of the burial: at Argos graves were cut into formerly inhabited areas, and parts of the cemetery were later built over (*DIPG* 24). See Dietz 1991, 275 for MH4, a cist grave cut into a wall of a house in the lower town at Asine; Dietz 1991, 292 for two shaft graves cut into the floor of an abandoned house in the Barbouna area of Asine. See also Nordquist 1987, 93; *DIPG* 25.

6 *BSA* 50, 207 (waterproofing, yellow-green clay); 208 (2 layers of green clay with red pebbly soil between them); 217 (layers of dark red, red, grey and green clay over the mound. All sherds below the clay MH–LH I).

7 *BSA* 62, 77–105; see also Tsountas 1885 cols. 35–42; Hammond 1976, 116; Pélon 1976, 148–52. The subject is well discussed by Dietz (*Asine II* 72–4).

8 Examples in the Citadel House Area would be Γ **Graves 5** and 6; **Grave 10**; **Grave 13**. See *DIPG* 26 for discussion.

9 For example, MH Grave I at Prosymna had small pieces of limestone laid along the west side of the pit to take cover slabs, although the slabs themselves were missing and the grave had been disturbed (*Prosymna*, 30). See also MH Grave XXVII (*Prosymna*, 46).

10 Cf. Grave 64 at Lerna: Blackburn 1970, 67; Argos, Tumulus B, Grave A (137), Protonariou-Deilaki 1980, 24–5, pl. B3,3; Argos Tumulus E Grave 3 (90): Protonariou-Deilaki 1980, 113 and pl. E2 1–3, and plan E3. The type is discussed by Nordquist 1987, 93.

11 Cf. Grave 85 at Lerna, where the decayed roof bricks were found in a crumbled mass.

12 As in Grave 109 at Lerna: Blackburn 1970, 99.

13 MH Grave IV at Prosymna was covered with a mass of small stones and earth: on top of the heap were four vases (*Prosymna*, 37).

14 As in Argos Tumulus Δ Grave 1 (140): Protonariou-Deilaki 1980, 91–101.

15 As Argos Tumulus Γ Burial 70 (Pithos 12): Protonariou-Deilaki 1980, 72 and pl. Γ 21, 5–6 and Γ26, 3.

16 Grave 1971–7 at Asine contained the burials of two women in a jar; Grave 1971–15 at the same site contained the burials of two adults in a jar: *Asine II* 58, 62; At Argos there were two skeletons in each of Tumulus A pithos grave 121 and Tumulus Γ pithos grave 69: Protonariou-Deilaki 1990a, 72 figs 3b and 3c.

17 Eg. Γ **Graves 7** and **9**: cf. the heap of bones between MH Graves VII and VIII at Prosymna (*Prosymna*, 39).

18 Like Grave 162 at Lerna: Blackburn 1970, 129. See also graves H, Z, I, and Ξ in Grave Circle B; Graziado 1991, 407.

19 Lerna Grave 136: Blackburn 1970, 116; Argos Tumulus Γ Grave 71 (13): Protonariou-Deilaki 1980, 77 and pl. Γ24, 3–4; 1990a, 81 fig. 26.

20   Cf. MH Grave XXI (A, B and C) at Prosymna (*Prosymna,* 42–3).

21   Thomas (1989, 105) suggests that the third generation was often the limit of a family's knowledge of its ancestors.

22   e.g. Ayioi Anargyroi (Naxos): Doumas 1977, 41 fig. 22, 101, and pl. XVII c, d, f, g.

23   *GCB* 112. For high pillows in Grave Circle A, see Tsountas and Manatt 1897, 95.

24   Vases were found before the face of burials in MH Graves XII, XV and XX at Prosymna (*Prosymna* 49, 40, 33); at Asine in Graves 1971–2 (*Asine II* 33–4) and B34 (*AAA* 8, 154–5); at Argos in Tumulus Γ Grave XIII (14), Grave 82 (23), Grave 83 (25), Tumulus Δ Grave 162 (3β) Tumulus E Grave 6 (93): Protonariou-Deilaki 1980, 41–2, 84, 85–6, 109, 119–21.

25   Graves 78, 99, 103, 121, 162: Blackburn 1970, 77, 92, 95, 105, 130: cf. MH Grave XI at Prosymna, where the shaft of the pin is bronze (*Prosymna,* 49).

26   Cf. Blackburn 1970, 11, and 111 for Lerna Grave 130; scattered bones of one individual disturbed from a grave of unknown location.

27   Cf. the three large stones in a row marking the position of Grave 167 at Lerna: Blackburn 1970, 133.

28   For brick-lined cists, see Blackburn 1970, 16 and 67 on Lerna grave 64; Protonariou-Deilaki 1980, 25 and fig. B3,3 on Argos tumulus B grave A (137) of brick with a timber and clay roof.

29   For roof bricks found in a crumbled mass over grave 85 at Lerna, see Blackburn 1970, 82–3.

30   Dr. David Heylings of the Department of Anatomy at the Queen's University of Belfast kindly drew my attention to the Spitalfields project.

31   Angel suggests that the bones of *148* and *149 Myc.* might belong to the same individual. It is certainly my opinion that they do.

32   The methods used to determine the number of children borne by a woman are suspect. The female pelvis often develops pits on the pubis symphysis and preauricular sulci where ligaments attach. These pits have been deemed a consequence of childbearing, but in fact they simply correlate with large pelvic dimensions. The findings of the Spitalfields project, where parish registers were available with details of births to the subjects examined, suggest that it is impossible to tell from the osteological evidence whether a woman has borne a child (Molleson and Cox 1993, 135–6 and 214).

BIBLIOGRAPHY AND SPECIAL ABBREVIATIONS

These include only those items which are new to this fascicule. References and abbreviations used in the introductory fascicule (*WBM* 1) are printed there on pp. 55–63. A consolidated bibliography for all fascicules will be published when the series is complete.

SPECIAL ABBREVIATIONS

AA	*Archäologischer Anzeiger*
AAA	*Ἀρχαιολογικά Ἀνάλεκτα ἐξ Ἀθηνῶν*
AJA	*American Journal of Archaeology*
Asine	Frödin, O. and Persson, A. W., *Asine: Results of the Swedish Excavations 1922–30*, Stockholm 1938.
Asine II	Dietz, S., *Asine II: Results of the Excavations East of the Acropolis 1970–74*, fasc. 1, Stockholm 1982; fasc. 2, *The Middle Helladic Cemetery, The Middle Helladic and Early Mycenaean Deposits*, Stockholm 1980.
Ath. Mitt.	*Athenische Mitteilungen*
BICS	*Bulletin of the Institute of Classical Studies*
Corinth XIII	Blegen, C. W., *Corinth XIII: the North Cemetery*, i. Princeton 1964.
Death and Divinity	Hägg, R. and Nordquist, G., *Celebrations of Death and Divinity in the Bronze Age Argolid*, Proceedings of the Sixth International Symposium at the Swedish Institute at Athens, 11–13 June 1988, Skrifter Utgivna av Svenska Insitutet i Athen 4°, XL, Stockholm.
DIPG	Cavanagh, W. and Mee, C., *A Private Place: Death in Prehistoric Greece*, SIMA 125, Jonsered 1998.
Eutresis	Goldman, H., *Excavations at Eutresis in Boeotia*, Cambridge, Mass. 1931.
Jahrbuch	*Jahrbuch des Deutschen Archäologischen Instituts, Berlin.*
JHS	*Journal of Hellenic Studies*
Korakou	Blegen, C. W., *Korakou: A Prehistoric Settlement near Corinth*, Boston and New York 1921.
Nichoria	McDonald, W. A. and Wilkie, N. C., *Excavations at Nichoria in Southwest Greece* ii: *The Bronze Age Occupation*, Minneapolis 1992.
Προϊστ. Ἐλευσίς	Mylonas, G. E. *Προϊστορική Ἐλευσίς*, Athens 1932.
Prosymna	Blegen, C. W., *Prosymna: the Helladic Settlement preceding the Argive Heraeum*, i and ii. Cambridge 1937.
RA	*Revue Archéologique*
SIMA	Studies in Mediterranean Archaeology
X-S	Κατάλογος διακοσμητικῶν θεμάτων κοσμημάτων, in Xenake-Sakellariou, A. *Οἱ Θαλαμωτοί Τάφοι τῶν Μυκηνῶν*, Paris 1985.
X-S 1995	Xenake-Sakellariou, A., 1985. *Οἱ Θαλαμωτοί Τάφοι τῶν Μυκηνῶν*, Paris.
Zygouries	Blegen, C. W., *Zygouries: A Prehistoric Settlement in the Vale of Cleonae*, Cambridge, Mass. 1928.

BIBLIOGRAPHY

Acsádi, G. and Nemeskéri, J.	1970	*History of human life span and mortality*, Budapest: Akadémiai Kiadó.
Alden, M. J.	1981	*Bronze Age Population Fluctuations in the Argolid from the Evidence of Mycenaean Tombs*, Gothenburg.
Angel, J. L.	1971	*The People of Lerna*, Princeton.
Antonaccio, C. M.	1993	'Tomb and Hero Cult in Early Greece: the Archaeology of Ancestors', in C. Dougherty and L. Kurke (eds.), *Cultural Poetics in Archaic Greece*, Cambridge.
Antonaccio, C. M.	1995	*An Archaeology of Ancestors: Tomb Cult and Hero Cult in Early Greece*, Lanham, Maryland.
Belger, C.	1895	'Erbauung und Zerstörung des mykenischen Plattenringes', *Jahrbuch* 10, 114–7.
Blackburn, E. Tucker,	1970	'Middle Helladic Graves and Burial Customs with Special Reference to Lerna and the Argolid', Cinncinati Ph.D thesis.
Blegen, C. W.	1921	*Korakou: A Prehistoric Settlement near Corinth*, Boston and New York, (abbreviated *Korakou*).
Blegen, C. W.	1928	*Zygouries: A Prehistoric Settlement in the Vale of Cleonae*, Cambridge, Mass, (abbreviated *Zygouries*).
Blegen, C. W.	1937	*Prosymna: the Helladic Settlement preceding the Argive Heraeum*, i and ii. Cambridge, (abbreviated *Prosymna*).
Blegen, C. W.	1964	*Corinth XIII: the North Cemetery*, i. Princeton, (abbreviated *Corinth XIII*).
Boardman, J.	1970	'The Danicourt Ring', *RA*, 3–8.
Branigan, K. (ed.)	1998	*Cemetery and Society in the Aegean Bronze Age*, Sheffield.
Caskey, M.	1971	'Newsletter from Greece', *AJA* 75, 305.
Cavanagh, W.	1978	'A Mycenaean Second Burial Custom?' *BICS* 25, 171–2.
Cavanagh, W. and Mee, C.	1998	*A Private Place: Death in Prehistoric Greece*, SIMA 125, Jonsered, (abbreviated *DIPG*).
Coldstream, J. N.	1973	*Knossos: the Sanctuary of Demeter*, BSA supplementary volume no. 8, London.
Demacopoulou, K.	1974	'Μυκηναϊκὸν ἀνακτορικὸν ἐργαστήριον εἰς Θήβας', *AAA* 7 pt. 2, 162–73.
Desborough, V. R. d'A.	1954	'Mycenae 1939–53, Part V: Four Tombs,' *BSA* 49, 258–9.
Dickinson, O. T. P. K.	1972	'Late Helladic IIA and IIB: Some Evidence from Korakou', *BSA* 67, 103–112.
Dickinson, O. T. P. K.	1974	'The Definition of Late Helladic I', *BSA* 69, 109–120.

Dickinson, O. T. P. K.	1977	*The Origins of Mycenaean Civilization*, SIMA 49, Gothenburg.
Dickinson, O. T. P. K.	1983	'Cist Graves and Chamber Tombs', *BSA* 78, 55–67.
Dietz, S.	1980	*Asine II: Results of the Excavations East of the Acropolis 1970–74*, fasc. 1, Stockholm 1982; fasc. 2, *The Middle Helladic Cemetery, The Middle Helladic and Early Mycenaean Deposits*, Stockholm, (abbreviated *Asine II*).
Dietz, S.	1991	*The Argolid at the Transition to the Mycenaean Age*, Copenhagen.
Doumas, C.	1977	*Early Bronze Age Burial Habits in the Cyclades*, SIMA 48, Gothenburg.
Evans, A. J.	1901	'Mycenaean Tree and Pillar Cult', *JHS* 21, 99–204.
Evans, A. J.	1921–35	*The Palace of Minos at Knossos*, i–iv. London.
Evans, A. J.	1929	*The Shaft Graves and Bee-hive Tombs of Mycenae*, London.
French, E. B. and Iakovides, S. E.	forthcoming	*The Mycenae Atlas,* Archaeological Society of Athens.
Frödin, O. and Persson, A. W.	1938	*Asine: Results of the Swedish Excavations 1922–30*, Stockholm, (abbreviated *Asine*).
Furumark, A.	1941*b*	*The Chronology of Mycenaean Pottery*, Stockholm.
Gates, C.	1985	'Rethinking the Building History of Grave Circle A at Mycenae', *AJA* 89, 263–9.
Gill, M. A. V.	1985	'L'iconographie Minoenne', *BCH* supp. 11, 78–9.
Goldman, H.	1931	*Excavations at Eutresis in Boeotia*, Cambridge, Mass, (abbreviated *Eutresis*).
Graziado, G.	1991	'The Process of Social Stratification at Mycenae in the Shaft Grave Period: A Comparative Examination of the Evidence', *AJA* 95, 403–40.
Grossmann, P. and Schaeffer, J.	1975	*Tiryns* viii: 'Tiryns: Unterburg 1968. Grabungen im Bereich der Bauten 3 und 4', Mainz.
Hägg, I. and Hägg, R.	1975	'Discoveries at Asine Dating from the Shaft-Grave Period', *AAA* 8, 151–60.
Hägg, R. and Nordquist, G. (eds.)	1990	*Celebrations of Death and Divinity in the Bronze Age Argolid*, Proceedings of the Sixth International Symposium at the Swedish Institute at Athens, 11–13 June 1988, Skrifter Utgivna av Svenska Insitutet i Athen 4°, XL, Stockholm, (abbreviated *Death and Divinity*).
Hamilakis, Y.	1998	'Eating the Dead: Mortuary Feasting and the Politics of Memory in the Aegean Bronze Age Societies', in K. Branigan (ed.), *Cemetery and Society in the Aegean Bronze Age*, Sheffield, 115–32.
Hammond, N. G. L.	1967	'Tumulus Burial in Albania, the Grave Circles of Mycenae, and the Indo-Europeans', *BSA* 62, 77–105.

Hammond, N. G. L.	1976	*Migrations and Invasions in Greece and Adjacent Areas*, Park Ridge N. J.
Harding, A. and Hughes-Brock, H.	1974	'Amber in the Mycenaean World', *BSA* 69, 145–72.
Haussoullier, B.	1878	'Catalogue descriptif des objets découverts à Spata', *BCH* 2, 184–228 and pls. 13–19.
Heurtley, W. A.	1921–23	'Mycenae. The Grave Stelai', *BSA* 25, 126–46.
Higgins, R. A.	1980	*Greek and Roman Jewellery*, London (first pub. 1961).
Hughes-Brock, H.	1973	'The Beads, Loomweights etc', in J. N. Coldstream, *Knossos: Sanctuary of Demeter.*
Hughes-Brock, H.	1985	'Amber and the Mycenaeans', *Journal of Baltic Studies* 16, 257–67.
Karo, G.	1915	'Die Schachtgräber von Mykenai', *Ath. Mitt.* 40, 113–230.
Karo, G.	1930–3	*Die Schachtgräber von Mykenai*, i and ii. Munich.
Keramopoullos, A.	1918	'Περὶ τῶν Βασιλικῶν Τάφων τῆς Ἀκροπόλεως τῶν Μυκηνῶν, *AE*, 52–60.
Kilian, K.	1979	'Ausgrabungen in Tiryns 1977', *AA,* 379–411.
Kilian-Dirlmeier, I.	1986	'Beobachtungen zu den Schactgräbern von Mykenai und zu den Schmuckbeigaben mykenischen Männer', *Jahrbuch des Römisch-Germanischen Zentralmuseums* 33, 156–86.
Kilian-Dirlmeier, I.	1989	'Οι Ταφικόι Κυκλόι Α και Β των Μυκηνών (μία σύγκριση)', *Πρακτικά του Β΄ Τοπικού Συνέδριου Αργολικών Σπουδών* (Ἄργος 30 Μαΐου–1 Ἰουνίου 1986), Athens, 167–76.
Koumanoudes, S. A.	1878	[Report on Mycenae], *PAE*, 25–6.
Kourouniotis, K.	1932	*Eleusiniaka*, Athens.
Krzyzkowska, O.	1988	'Ivory in the Aegean Bronze Age: Elephant Tusk or Hippopotamus Ivory?', *BSA* 83, 209–34
Laffineur, R.	1990	'Grave Circle A at Mycenae: Further Reflections on its History', in *Death and Divinity*, 201–5.
Lolling, H. G.	1880	*Das Kuppelgrab bei Menidi*, Athens.
Lolling, H. G. and Wolters, P.	1886	'Das Kuppelgrab bei Dimini', *Ath. Mitt.* 11, 435–43.
Lolling, H. G. and Wolters, P.	1887	'Das Kuppelgrab bei Dimini II', *Ath. Mitt.* 12, 136–8.
McDonald, W. *et al.*	1975	'Excavations at Nichoria in Messenia', *Hesperia* 44, 73–5.
Marinatos, S.	1953	'Περὶ τοὺς νέους βασιλικοὺς τάφους τῶν Μυκηνῶν' in *Γέρας Ἀντώνιου Κεραμοπούλλου*, Ἑταιρεία Μακεδωνικῶν Σπουδῶν 9, Athens, 54–88 and pls. 6–9.

Marinatos, S.	1967	'Kleidung, Haar- und Bartracht', *Archaeologica Homerica* i, Göttingen.
McDonald, W. A. and Wilkie, N. C.	1992	*Excavations at Nichoria in Southwest Greece* ii: *The Bronze Age Occupation*, Minneapolis, (abbreviated *Nichoria*).
Milchhöfer, A.	1876	'Die Ausgrabungen in Mykene', *Ath. Mitt.* 1, 309–27.
Molleson, T. and Cox, M.	1993	*The Spitalfields Project* ii. *The Anthropology: The Middling Sort.* Council for British Archaeology Report 86.
Morris, S. P.	1984	*The Black and White Style: Athens and Aigina in the Orientalizing Period*, Yale.
Müller, K.	1915	'Frühmykenische Reliefs. II. Das Griechische Festland', *Jahrbuch* 30, 284–94.
Mylonas, G. E.	1932	Προϊστορικὴ Ἐλευσίς, Athens, (abbreviated Προϊστ. Ἐλευσίς).
Mylonas, G. E.	1951	'The figured Mycenaean Stelai', *AJA* 55, 134–47.
Mylonas, G. E.	1951	'The Cult of the Dead in Helladic Times', in G. E. Mylonas (ed.), *Studies Presented to David M. Robinson*, St. Louis, 64–105.
Mylonas, G. E.	1958*a*	Ἡ ἀκρόπολις τῶν Μυκηνῶν', *AE,* 153–207.
Mylonas, G. E.	1958*b*	'The Grave Circles of Mycenae', *Minoica*: Festschrift zum 80. Geburtstag von Johannes Sundwall, Berlin, 276–86 and pl. 1.
Mylonas, G. E.	1959	*Aghios Kosmas: An Early Bronze Age Settlement and Cemetery in Attica*, Princeton.
Mylonas, G. E.	1962	Ἡ ἀκρόπολις τῶν Μυκηνῶν. Μέρος δεύτερον. Οἱ περίβολοι, αἱ πύλαι καὶ αἱ ἄνοδοι', *AE,* 1–199.
Mylonas, G. E.	1972–3	Ὁ Ταφικός Κύκλος Β τῶν Μυκηνῶν, Athens.
Mylonas, G. E.	1973	'Μυκῆναι', *Ergon,* 66–79.
Mylonas, G. E. and Iakovides, S. E.	1984	'Ἀνάσκαφη Μυκηνῶν', *PAE,* 233–40.
Niemeier, W.-D.	1990	'Cult Scenes on Gold Rings from the Argolid', in *Death and Divinity,* 165–70.
Nilsson, M. P.	1950	*The Minoan-Mycenaean Religion and its Survival in Greek Religion*, Lund.
Nordquist, G. C.	1987	'A Middle Helladic Village: Asine in the Argolid', *Boreas* 16, 91–195, (Uppsala Studies in Ancient Mediterranean and Near Eastern Civilization, Uppsala).
Nordquist, G. C.	1990	'Middle Helladic Burial Rites: Some Speculations', in *Death and Divinity,* 36–43.
Onasoglou, A.	1995	Ἡ οἰκία τοῦ τάφου τῶν τρίποδων στις Μυκῆνες, Βιβλιοθήκη τῆς ἐν Ἀθηναῖς Ἀρχαιολογικῆς Ἑταιρείας no. 147.

Papademetriou, I.	1955	'Ἀνασκαφαὶ ἐν Μυκήναις', *PAE*, 217–32.
Papademetriou, I.	1957	'Ἀνασκαφαὶ ἐν Μυκήναις', *PAE*, 105–9.
Pélon, O.	1976	*Tholoi, Tumuli, et Cercles Funéraires: recherches sur les monuments funéraires de plan circulaire dans l'Egée á l'âge du Bronze (IIIe et IIe millénaires avant J.C.)* École Française d'Athènes, Paris.
Perrot, G. and Chipiez, C.	1894	*Histoire de l'Art dans l'Antiquité*, vi: *La Grèce Primitive, L'Art Mycenien*, Paris.
Popham, M. R. and Catling, E. A. and H. W.	1974	'Sellopoulo Tombs 3 and 4: Two Late Minoan Graves near Knossos', *BSA* 69, 195–257.
Protonariou-Deilaki, E.	1980	*Οἱ Τύμβοι τοῦ Ἄργους*, Ἄργος 1, Athens.
Protonariou-Deilaki, E.	1990*a*	'Burial Customs and Funerary Rites in the Prehistoric Argolid', in *Death and Divinity*.
Protonariou-Deilaki, E.	1990*b*	'The Tumuli of Mycenae and Dendra', in *Death and Divinity*.
Catling, E. A. and H. W.		Graves near Knossos', *BSA* 69, 195–257.
Prag, A. J. N. W. *et al.*	1995	'Seven Faces from Grave Circle B at Mycenae', *BSA* 90, 107–36 and pls. 14–18.
Rawson, M., Taylour Lord William, and Donovan, W. P.	1973	*Pylos* iii: *The Palace of Nestor at Pylos in Western Messenia*, Princeton.
Reichel, W.	1893	'Die Mykenische Grabstelen', *Eranos Vindobonensis*, Vienna, 24–33.
Schaeffer, C. F. A.	1952	*Enkomi-Alasia*, Paris.
Shear, T. L.	1940	'Excavations in the Athenian Agora: the Campaign of 1939', *Hesperia* 9, 261–307.
Schuchhardt, C.	1891	*Schliemann's Excavations*, London, reissued New York 1971.
Staïs, B.	1915	*Collection Mycénienne du Musée Nationale²*, ii. Athens.
Spyropoulos, T.	1971	'Preliminary report of excavations at Paralimni', *AAA* 4, 319–31.
Theochare, M. A.	1962	'Δοκιμαστικὴ ἀνάσκαφη εἰς Χασαμπαλι Λάρισης', *Thessalika* 4, 35–50.
Thomas, H.	1938–9	'The Acropolis Treasure from Mycenae', *BSA* 39, 65–87.
Thomas, R.	1989	*Oral Tradition and Written Record in Classical Athens*, Cambridge.
Tournavitou, I.	1995	'The Ivory Houses at Mycenae', *BSA*, Suppl. vol. 24.
Tsountas, C.	1885	'Οἱ Προϊστορικοὶ Τάφοι τῆς Ἑλλάδος', *AE* col. 34–42.
Tsountas, C.	1893	*Μυκῆναι καὶ Μυκηναῖος Πολιτισμός*, Athens.
Tsountas, C.	1895	'Zu einigen mykenischen Streitfragen', *Jahrbuch* 10, 143–51.

Tsountas, C.	1897	'Μῆτραι καὶ ξίφη ἐκ Μυκηνῶν', *AE*, 98–128 and pls. 7–8.
Valmin, N.	1938	*The Swedish Messenian Expedition*, Lund.
Vermeule, E. T.	1967	'A Mycenaean Jeweler's Mold', *Bulletin of Boston Museum of Fine Arts* 65, 19–31.
Vollgraff, W.	1906	'Fouilles d'Argos', *Bulletin de Correspondance Héllenique* 30, 12–14.
Wace, A. J. B. and Blegen, C. W.	1930	'Middle Helladic Tombs', *Symbolae Osloenses* 9, 28–37.
Wace, A. J. B.	1956	'Mycenae 1939–1955. Part II. Ephyraean Ware', *BSA* 51, 123–7.
Wolters, P.	1889	'Mykenische Vasen aus dem nördlichen Griechenland', *Ath. Mitt.* 14, 262–70.
Xenake-Sakellariou, A.	1985	*Οἱ Θαλαμωτοί Τάφοι τῶν Μυκηνῶν*, Paris, (abbreviated *X-S 1995*).
Younger, J. G.	1984	'Aegean Seals of the Late Bronze Age: Masters and Workshops III. The first generation Mycenaean masters', *Kadmos* 23, 58–60.